Quiet
Kids

Help Your Introverted Child
Succeed in an Extroverted World

Quiet Kids

Christine Fonseca

PRUFROCK PRESS INC.
WACO, TEXAS

Dedicated to the introverts
in my own life who made my own
sense of silence so much more powerful.

Library of Congress Cataloging-in-Publication Data

Fonseca, Christine, 1966-
Quiet kids : help your introverted child succeed in an extroverted world / by Christine
Fonseca.
    pages cm
Includes bibliographical references.
ISBN 978-1-61821-082-1 (pbk.)
1. Introversion in children. 2. Child rearing. I. Title.
BF723.I68F66 2013
155.4'18232--dc23
                        2013019016

Edited by Lacy Compton

Cover and layout design by Raquel Trevino

ISBN-13: 978-1-61821-082-1

Prufrock Press Inc.
P.O. Box 8813
Waco, TX 76714-8813
Phone: (800) 998-2208
Fax: (800) 240-0333
http://www.prufrock.com

Table of Contents

Acknowledgements

I am an introverted adult, and, as such, I have had to learn how to harness the strength within my need for silence. I couldn't have learned how to draw on my own unique strengths without the team of people that regularly draw me from my shell and encourage me to share my knowledge with the world. And while I am certain this list is incomplete, here are a few of the people who have shaped this book and helped to make it more than I thought possible.

I couldn't have developed the ideas and this book without the encouragement and guidance of my editor, Lacy Compton. She is a constant support to me, shaping and guiding each and every title she convinces me to write. The teams at Prufrock Press and Sourcebooks continue her support and turn my ideas into something amazing.

My writing partner, Michelle McLean, an introvert herself, is always willing to tell it like it is and force me to go deeper in my work. Thank you for last-minute reading and lending your stories and support.

My writing buddies, Elana Johnson, Ali Cross, and Dustin Hansen—without all of you I would have avoided this book altogether. Thank you for never letting me off the hook and forcing me to sit in the chair and pound this out! Your tweets got me through it all!

To my RL BFFs and cheer squad: Jodi, Stephanie, Jill, Judy, Corrine, Shauna, and Andrea—You all listen when I need to share, give me the quiet I need to renew, and understand the "me" inside. Your friendship means more than I could ever express. No matter how our lives change over the next few years, let's continue to commit to carve out time for each other!

The endless sea of support from the writing community, the bloggers, readers, and fangirls I never dreamed I'd have—although I've never met the majority of you in person, you all mean the world to me. Your encouragement and understanding of the industry we all love is nothing short of amazing.

Finally, my acknowledgements are never complete without a personal thank you to my family, both immediate and extended. Dirck, Fabiana, and Erika—you three are the best cheerleaders and support team anyone could ever wish for. You work together to keep things running smoothly, no matter how stressed I get with my deadlines. "Thank you" seems too inadequate a word to capture the depth of my gratitude. Debra, Daryn, Karol, Vince, Errol, Celia—you are all so supportive and "get" me and my crazy need to write. Dad, Trudy, and Virginia—you know and understand the deepest aspects of who I am, and you are always around with encouragement when I need it the most. Thank you to all of you for everything you mean in my life!

—Christine Fonseca

Author's Note

I remember the day the ideas for *Quiet Kids* started to gel in my head. Temperament has long been a part of the content in my speaking and coaching work, and something that people resonate toward in their questions and e-mails. As an introverted adult, I understand the impact my own introversion has had in my life. I know, firsthand, the information I wish my parents knew; the information they would have liked to have taught me. I remember watching my mom struggle with her own misconceptions about her introverted nature. And I remember my confusion as I tried, unsuccessfully, to turn myself into a social butterfly in a way that contradicted my own hardwiring. It is with these memories and thoughts that this book was written, each page and chapter crafted to inform and inspire parents as they work to help their introverted children thrive in a world that cherishes extroversion and often mislabels the introvert.

This book is filled with personal stories from my own life, as well as from the lives of people who have shared a snippet of their worlds with me during speaking engagements, coaching sessions, and through the focus groups I held as I researched the book. I have purposefully changed the names and identifying information in this book, as many of these individuals shared stories without realizing I would one day write a book on the topic. And although the stories are altered from their original form somewhat, they serve to illustrate the ups and downs of introverted children, and the challenges many parents and educators face when working with them.

My hope is that *Quiet Kids* will illuminate the strengths that exist within the introverted temperament and enable you to teach your children how to embrace their own silence and nurture this aspect of themselves.

—Christine Fonseca

Introduction

A young boy starts third grade filled with excitement. He walks into the class, not knowing anyone. Somewhat intimidated, he pulls away from the other kids, watching as the other students answer the teacher's questions. He seldom participates and is considered by the teacher as having a quiet temperament, too quiet. After a few weeks, the teacher grows concerned that the young boy may have learning difficulties. She calls a meeting with the parent, only to discover that the child has never struggled in school previously. The teacher quizzes the student on the current material and discovers that the young boy does know the material—all of the material. Perplexed, the teacher and parent begin to worry that something is "wrong" with the little boy.

Miles away, in a different state, a teenage girl sits with her friends at a local coffee house. She has received the wrong order. But, instead of letting the barista know, she just gives her drink to someone else and pushes aside her frustration with not being able to ask the barista for her correct order. *I'm so stupid. I hate being so shy*, she says to herself as an overwhelming shame creeps into her thoughts.

A few tables away, a group of middle school kids laugh and joke around with each other. That is, all except for one 13-year-old boy. He appears to be distracted, starring off into space. His friends try to engage him in conversation, but he is too lost in his thoughts to notice. After several minutes, one of his friends snaps his fingers in front of the boy's face, determined to draw his attention. The boy snaps, yelling at the others before leaving the coffee house, frustrated.

Each of these scenarios has something in common. They each feature an introverted child struggling to understand that aspect of his or her nature. And in most cases, the other people involved will misunderstand what has happened as well and form a negative opinion of the child—one that is seldom true.

The terms *introversion* and *extroversion* are not new. Most people realize that these terms refer to temperament. However, every time I ask audiences to give me a definition for these words, I get the following list of attributes:

Introverted:

❖ Shy
❖ Lonely
❖ Withdrawn
❖ Depressed
❖ Self-centered

Extroverted:

❖ Outgoing
❖ Popular
❖ Likes to be part of a group
❖ Happy
❖ Active

These lists paint introversion in a predominantly negative light, while painting extroversion as something worthy of aspiration. It is a belief representative of our current cultural norms that celebrate extroversion as *the* ideal, something we must nurture and encourage in our own children.

What the list fails to recognize is that temperament, like eye color and physical build, is hardwired. It is neither good nor bad, merely an aspect of who we are. And like most aspects of being, temperament brings with it its own strengths and potential problems.

As I mentioned earlier, we live in a world "built" for the extrovert. Our educational system favors group work and collaboration. Our business culture is heavily focused on collaborative innovation. And our pop culture favors those entertainers who court public attention.

What does this mean for the introverts? Are they supposed to simply alter their DNA in order to fit into the cultural norms? Suppress their need for quiet in favor of social prowess and an outgoing disposition? Is it even possible for them to do this?

I have a different idea. Designed to provide support to parents of introverted children, *Quiet Kids* pulls from current research and redefines introversion as something positive. It sheds light on the strengths of a quiet temperament, as well as providing parents and educators with specific strategies designed to help children embrace their introversion and develop their full potential. Presented in a readable and practical format, this book uses stories from other families of introverts, as well as practical workbook-style tasks and a Q&A section within each chapter to provide you with the tools you need to make a lasting positive impact on your child.

Quiet Kids addresses:

❖ society's assumptions about introversion and extroversion;
❖ the science behind temperament;
❖ working with introversion at school, at home, and with friends;
❖ specific strategies addressing resiliency, school performance, and living in a competitive culture; and
❖ how introversion plays out in the educational setting.

How to Use This Book

Quiet Kids, like my other nonfiction titles, is designed as a resource for parents and educators. Each section begins with an overview and self-reflection guide geared toward preparing you for the upcoming chapters. The sections end with a real-world story of an introvert related to the concepts presented within the section.

The chapters are set up to include tip sheets, as well as checklists and workbook-style tasks for use with parents and children as a way to enhance the material. The Q&A section presented at the end of the chapters address the more common questions I've been asked through focus groups and workshops on the topic of introversion. The chapters also end with a bullet-pointed "In a Nutshell" overview of the chapter, for ease of reference once the book has been read. The Recommended Resources section at the end of the book provides additional resources for the different topics that may arise as you work through the book.

A Word to Educators

This book was originally designed for use by parents. However, as I completed the focus groups and research for the book, it became clear that more resources were needed for educators and other professionals working with introverted children.

The concepts within each chapter have been retooled to address the classroom environment and are presented within the "Class Notes" sections. It is my hope that together, educators and parents can help introverted children embrace their unique nature and see their quiet demeanor as something positive and powerful.

part 1

Introverted and Extroverted Kids

A Matter of Hardwiring

Look up synonyms for extroverted on Thesaurus.com, and you will find words like *friendly*, *gregarious*, *social*, and *personable*. Look, instead, for synonyms for introverted, and you will find the words *shy*, *cold*, *secretive*, and *withdrawn*. These synonyms represent a list of attributes and behaviors that, at first glance, appear to be something we can choose, something we can change. Furthermore, there is a clear positive and negative connotation to the words, reflecting Western culture's favoring of extroversion.

But extroversion and introversion are more than a collection of attributes and behaviors that can be easily changed. These terms refer to our biological temperament. And although the more difficult aspects of each trait can be balanced, human beings are predisposed to particular temperaments. It is part of our hardwiring.

Over the next few chapters, I will examine the current neuroscience behind temperament, as well as the pros and cons of both extroversion and introversion. These chapters also take a hard look at the way society has depicted introversion and the impact this has on those hardwired to be more quiet than their extroverted counterparts.

As we begin this exploration into temperament, I think it's good to get clear on your own opinions about introversion and some of the concerns you have about raising an introverted child. Take a moment to complete the questionnaire on page 3 before moving into the next chapters.

QUESTIONNAIRE 1

Ideas About Temperament

1. I define an extroverted person as . . . (*complete the sentence*).

2. I define an introverted person as . . . (*complete the sentence*).

3. I believe that temperament is something you are born with.
   ❑ *True*   ❑ *False*

4. I believe that temperament can be changed over time.
   ❑ *True*   ❑ *False*

5. I think the world is more geared toward extroverts.
   ❑ *True*   ❑ *False*

6. If I answered "true" to #5, I think the biggest difficulties facing introverts are . . . (*complete the sentence*).

Once you are finished, take a moment to reflect on your answers and consider the following questions: What are the reasons you picked up this book? What are you hoping to get out of it? In what ways are you hoping to help your children? Take a moment to write down your thoughts regarding temperament and your goals for this book.

chapter 1

The Science of Temperament

"Temperament—what does that even mean? I just know that I am shy and quiet. It isn't something I think about. It is just part of who I am, something I accept as being me."
—Hiro, Age 15

Personality and temperament—two words that have come to be used interchangeably in our culture, but words that have significantly different meanings. Defined by Dictionary.com as being a collection of behaviors that form a person's character, personality is often influenced by both environmental considerations and things we experience in life. Temperament, on the other hand, is defined as being the traits affecting behavior that a person has at birth. It is shaped by biology and remains relatively unchanged throughout life.

Let me give you an example from my own life. When I was young, I was shy and reserved. I hated the first day of school, hated going someplace new, and struggled when I had to perform. However, my interests included music, dance, and modeling—every one of which required me to do something in front of an audience. These interests mandated that I get over my fear of performing in public. And I did. As an adult, I no longer fear being in front of large groups of people. I find comfort in speaking in front of hundreds of people at a time and no longer struggle with being the center of attention.

But I still get anxious when trying something new. I still consider myself reserved. And I continue to develop a little nausea at the thought of attending a conference with unfamiliar people. That part of me will never change.

So what's the difference between the two? Why has one aspect of me changed but the other one has not? It is the difference between personality traits and my temperament.

The fear of performing relates to my early feelings of being shy, something that changed through practice and experience. It is, or was, part of my personality. On the other hand, the continuing feeling of apprehension when confronted with something new is part of my temperament. It hasn't "matured" out of my behavior because it is a natural aspect of who I am. It is part of my hardwiring.

Personality and temperament. Nurture and nature.

Where do the concepts of extroversion and introversion fall into this mix? Often defined by specific behavioral characteristics (outgoing, social, and popular for extroverts, and quiet, shy, and reserved for introverts), these two concepts have long been accepted as part of a person's personality (Thompson, 2008). Popularly used by psychologist Carl Jung in the 1900s, these terms have found their way into nearly every discussion of personality, from Freud's somewhat negative view that introversion relates to narcissism, to Cattell's more neutral inclusion of extraversion and introversion as part of his 16 personality factors (Cattell, Eber, & Tatsuoka, 1980). Personality tests, including the Myers-Briggs Type Indicator and the Minnesota Multiphasic Personality Inventory, regularly include measures for extraversion (another spelling for extroversion) and introversion, using their scales to differentiate temperament in some way. Clearly, psychologists have recognized extroversion and introversion as aspects of temperament and personality throughout modern psychology. But it is the advancements in the field of neurobiology that has yielded the largest gains in our understanding of the field.

Jung (1971) long suspected a biological connection, believing that extroversion and introversion were things that related to how a person interacted with the world at a primal level, and not simply a by-product of the experiences a person has had. He believed that extroverts and introverts fundamentally viewed the world differently, with extroverts seeking stimulation outside of themselves, and introverts seeking internal stimulation.

Further evidence of a likely biological connection in the formation of temperament came from Segal's (1999) research on identical twins. After studying groups of twins raised apart, startling similarities were indicated with regard to temperament, regardless of the differences in environments in which the twins were raised (Segal, 1999).

Eysenck (1967), too, believed that temperament was a matter of biology. He believed that the differences between extroversion and introversion lay in the brain chemistry systems involving arousal and inhibition, with extroverts relying more heavily on arousal for balance and introverts being inhibition dominant. Although advancements in neuroscience have shown his work to be incomplete and somewhat oversimplistic, Eysenck's speculation that extroverts and introverts differ with reference to optimal level of arousal and reaction to environmental stimuli is basically correct.

Some of the most powerful research to recently address temperament and extroversion and introversion comes from Kagan's work (Kagan & Snidman, 2004) with highly sensitive children. In this research, Kagan studied brain chemistry and the role of neurotransmitters on temperament. He postulated that a child's genetic code determines how neurotransmitters are used and that this preference in the brain was intrinsically linked to temperament (Kagan & Snidman, 2004).

Perhaps the best understanding of the science behind temperament is explained by Marti Olsen Laney (2002) in *The Introvert Advantage*. Using the work of Kagan, as well as the neurotransmitter research conducted by Hobson, Kosslyn, and others, Laney (2002) described the differences between extroversion and introversion as being a matter of energy usage. Extroverts, Laney explained, use energy widely, while introverts are more likely to conserve it. Laney goes on to cite both the use of neurotransmitters as well as the activation and utilization of the sympathetic and para-sympathetic nervous systems as linked to extroversion and introversion.

Now, before you feel like you just woke up in the middle of your college biology class, I have no intention of repeating what Laney so elegantly explained in *The Introvert Advantage*. Instead I want to focus on what the recent research may mean for you, and, more importantly, for your children.

The chart in Figure 1 summarizes the work of Kagan, Laney, and others and shows at a glance just how different the hardwiring is for extroverts and introverts. It's no wonder neither group can fully understand the other—they are biologically different in their approach to life.

Brain chemistry controls how we behave in various situations. The research discussed in *The Introvert Advantage* points to something Jung (1971) had speculated about so much earlier—extroverts and introverts do, in fact, process energy differently. Extroverts focus on social connections and action as a path toward balanced brain arousal, while introverts look inward, preferring internal thinking as a path toward balance (Laney, 2002). It's something we are born with, and although we may find ways to neutralize the more extreme aspects of our temperament, at least where extroversion and introversion are involved, I believe we are largely dominant in one or the other.

So what's the main take-away here? Temperament is a function of nature. And the attributes of extroversion and introversion, as aspects of temperament, are the result of biology. They both have advantages and disadvantages. Although the negative aspects of either one can be mediated through some environmental and behavioral changes, the basic attributes of extroversion and introversion will remain true for you and your children throughout your lifetime.

Think back to the example I gave you of my own life. Although I have learned to overcome my childhood shyness when it came to performing and speaking, my natural reservation at trying something new and the apprehension I feel when starting an unfamiliar task will never disappear. It is part of my hardwiring.

In the next chapter, we'll examine the actual attributes of extroversion and introversion, as well as some of the problems that can arise with both when we are not in balance. But before we dive into that, I want

The Biological Differences Between Extroverts and Introverts

This chart shows a few of the biological and resultant behavioral differences between extroverts and introverts.

	Extroverts	*Introverts*
Neurotransmitter preference (Laney, 2002)	Dopamine—short and quick release system	Acetylcholine—long and slow release system
Arousal pattern	Seeks stimulation from the environment	Seeks stimulation through inner thoughts
Energy usage	Renews energy through connections and activity	Renews energy through internal thoughts and solitude
Nervous system activation (Laney, 2002)	Sympathetic ("fight or flight")—Promotes activation of the adrenal system in preparation for action.	Parasympathetic ("rest and digest")—Promotes the synthesis of glycogen and digestion.

Figure 1. Extroverts and introverts: A difference in biology.

you and every member of your household to complete the worksheet on page 10. Designed to help you identify the dominant temperaments of every member of your family, this is not a scientifically designed rating scale, but rather a collection of questions designed to help you determine where your innate traits may lie on the continuum.

Class Notes: Recognizing Temperament in the Classroom

You've all seen it before, the differences in the students in a typical classroom. Some will volunteer answers readily and love to participate in group activities. Others act as though a group project is a death sentence. As an educator, you know that you need to tailor your teaching to meet the needs of your students, coaching the quiet kids to speak out more and teaching the talkative ones to allow others to speak. It's a balancing act, to be certain.

WORKSHEET 1

Understanding My Child's Temperament (and My Own)

Directions: Read each of the 20 statements and determine if you agree, disagree, or neither. Complete the worksheet for each member of the household, including yourself. If your children are old enough, have them complete the worksheet as well as compare your results.

	I agree	I disagree	I neither agree nor disagree
1. I like talking with people after a long day.			
2. I prefer to spend time alone or with few friends.			
3. I get sad when I am alone for too long.			
4. When I make friends, I make deep friendships.			
5. I usually act first, and think second.			
6. I prefer to observe new situations before participating in them.			
7. I am very talkative.			
8. I need to feel comfortable before I will share information with people.			
9. I get hyper after fun activities.			
10. I typically think before I act.			
11. I have no problem talking with strangers.			
12. I really "faze out" when I am around large groups for too long.			
13. I appear to have a lot of energy.			

WORKSHEET 1, CONTINUED

	I agree	I disagree	I neither agree nor disagree
14. People say I often start talking in the middle of my thoughts.			
15. Most people think I have a lot of friends.			
16. I listen more than I talk.			
17. I don't like it when things are too predictable.			
18. I share my deepest fears with few people (or no one)			
19. I love going to parties and hanging out with friends.			
20. Being creative is important to me.			

Take a look at your answers. The even statements usually relate to introversion, the odd to extroversion. Looking at the chart, where are you dominant? It is important to note that these statements reflect general predictors of temperament. Most people will not fit neatly into a temperament label. Some extroverts may enjoy solitary activities like reading, while some introverts may thrive in the performing arts. Use these statements as guidelines to help you determine which side of the extroversion/introversion coin applies to you and your children the majority of the time. Repeat this for each of the members of the household. Any surprises?

In current Western educational institutions, collaboration and group activities have become the norm, the "best" type of learning for our students. You know that some of your students don't thrive with that structure of learning; maybe you've even found ways to accommodate them. But the message in education is clear; students need to learn how to work in teams. After all, our modern culture demands this of us.

But how does the introvert fit into this picture?

This chapter has focused on the biological differences between extroversion and introversion, highlighting a fundamental difference in how these two temperaments approach their interactions with the environment. As an educator, it is time to take this information and apply it to the classroom, understanding that the shy child who is reluctant to join groups, no matter how much you encourage him, may not be just "shy." He may be hardwired differently and require a different approach to learning.

More on that later in the book.

For now, I want you to take the information in the chapter and apply it to the classroom, using a similar worksheet to the one for parents as a way to recognize and identify temperament in your classroom (see p. 13). Use it with any student and enhance your ability to tailor some of your methodologies to the students in your class. Use it with yourself to more deeply understand why you may be energized and/or drained at the end of the day.

TEMPERAMENT Q&A

After reading about the physiology of temperament, you likely have a few questions. Trust me, you are not alone. Here are some questions frequently asked in my focus groups and workshops whenever the subject of temperament is mentioned.

WORKSHEET 2

Understanding My Students' Temperaments (and My Own)

Directions: Read and think about each of the 10 statements as they relate to your students. Complete one worksheet for each student. Or have your students complete it for themselves.

	I agree	I disagree	I neither agree nor disagree
1. I like talking with people after a long day.			
2. I prefer to spend time alone or with few friends.			
3. I like to volunteer in class.			
4. It takes me a while to warm up to a new teacher or a new class.			
5. I usually act first, and think second.			
6. I prefer to observe new situations before participating in them.			
7. I am very talkative.			
8. I need to feel comfortable before I will share information with people.			
9. I get hyper after fun activities.			
10. I typically think before I act.			

Take a look at the answers. The even statements related to introversion, the odd relate to extroversion. Remember, these are just general predictors. Most students will have attributes of both temperaments. Use the chart to assess your students' temperament trends and assist in assessing needs. Looking at the chart, where are your students dominant? Do this for the majority of your students. If you are like most environments, you will find a higher number of extroverts in your classroom. What have you learned?

You stated that introverts and extroverts are hardwired differently. Is this something that can change over time, like with age?

Yes and no. Like anything with our physiology, there are seldom easy answers. Everything is a balance between our hardwiring and our learned patterns of response.

I believe we have a predisposition toward a specific pattern of responding to our environment. In the case of an introverted person, he may always have a physical reaction when asked to answer a question in class or when put on the spot in a business meeting. He may also prefer to think through a problem before acting on it. He may always appear to be tired or "tuned-out" when in crowds for extended periods of time. But how he responds to those initial reactions is likely to change over time. Whereas he may have responded to being in a crowd or being called on in class by withdrawing, being quiet, or becoming physically ill when he was a child, now he responds by taking a deep breath, clearing his thoughts, and talking himself through his feelings. He appears to have minimized his introversion. In fact, the introversion hasn't changed at all. It is merely his reactions to his biology that have changed over time.

Can someone be both extroverted and introverted, depending on the situation?

There are some psychological studies that have utilized the term *ambivert* to refer to persons who reflect both extroverted and introverted qualities. They are in the "middle" of the continuum between the two. Before you run off and decide this applies to you, I want to offer you a different opinion. I believe, like Jung, that all human beings possess qualities of both extroversion and introversion. But I also believe that we have a dominant temperament related to our brain chemistry, our use of the autonomic nervous system, and our reaction to various neurotransmitters. In that respect, I would say "no," you are not extroverted or introverted based on a given situation.

So how do you figure out what is dominant for you or your children? Think back to a time when you were emotionally spent. What did you crave in that moment? Solitude? Time to think, process, or reflect? Or did you want to talk with a friend? Go to a social activity? Run and be active? The answer to these questions can help you determine your dominance—introversion or extroversion.

Is it possible to be too introverted?

Like any aspect of being, too much of something is often not a good thing. When introverts are overwhelmed and out of balance, they have a tendency to fully withdraw from the world. They can become distant, appear unmotivated to complete preferred tasks, and even seem depressed. Their biology, the parts related to introversion, are overactivated, resulting in brain chemistry that is out of sync. The same can happen when an extrovert becomes overstimulated by her dominant brain chemistry, resulting in myriad health problems related to an overexcited stress response.

The key to all of this is learning how to balance the dominant neurology, thereby avoiding the potential pitfalls. I will speak more to this throughout the book, including tips for helping introverted children avoid becoming out of sync.

The chart really clarifies the biological differences between introverts and extroverts. Are there some physical indicators that you have noticed personally that informed you of your temperament?

Ah yes, my personal dealings with my biology. I think the most prominent physical indicators of my introversion come when I am experiencing some form of overload—when the noise and demands of the environment surpass my immediate coping strategies. I literally feel like someone is raking 9-inch nails down my arm when I am overwhelmed. My skin hurts, my ears pound, and I literally can't think. I can become short-tempered and overly quick to react in a negative way.

I have come to realize that this physical reaction is related to anxiety and stress—both of which are more likely to occur when my system is taxed related to my introversion. Some of the other behavioral characteristics of introversion are covered in the next chapter, as we discuss the specific attributes and characteristics of introversion.

As I am a teacher, I find this information interesting, but not necessarily helpful. How can I use the science of temperament in my daily functioning as an educator?

Understanding temperament can not only enhance your understanding of your students, but can change both your approach to teaching and your understanding of the behavioral nuances you see in your class. The child who refuses to answer questions aloud or stares off into space whenever the noise in the room gets a little louder is no longer a student who is disinterested in learning, poorly motivated, or even learning disabled. Armed with this information, you can now see that the student may, in fact, be hardwired in a way that is contradictory to your class environment or teaching strategies. This understanding will enable you to probe a little deeper and try a few different environmental changes before assuming the student struggles with learning or motivation.

The most important thing the information in this chapter can give you is the gift of tolerance. With a broad and accepting lens, you can view the student's behavior in a more neutral light, understanding that the behavioral nuances you are observing are not just a choice the student is making, but so much more. And that can make a world of difference for the child.

In the following chapters, I will go more deeply into the actual differences between extroversion and introversion. Until then, try your hand at beginning to recognize the subtle differences yourself.

In a Nutshell . . .

Big Ideas
- ❖ Temperament is a matter of hardwiring.
- ❖ Extroverts and introverts respond differently to external and internal stimuli.
- ❖ Extroverts and introverts utilize their autonomic nervous system differently.

❖ Extroverts and introverts use and react to neurotransmitters differently.

❖ Temperament is only one aspect of who we are. Neither extroverts nor introverts are exactly like one another.

Supplemental Pages

chapter 2

A Wallflower? Or Not?

"I feel bad that I am not as social as my friends. But being reserved doesn't mean there is something wrong with me. I wish more people understood that."—Emma, Age 10

In the last chapter, we started our conversation about the biological differences between extroverted and introverted children in terms of energy usage, neurotransmitter dependence, and nervous system functioning. How does this translate to behavior and overall functioning? What does this actually mean for the child?

Extroverts and introverts interact with the world in different and unique ways, including the ways in which they communicate, how they restore their energy reserves, and how they generally behave. Let's look at each one of these areas one at a time.

I mentioned previously that extroverts are outgoing and talkative. This is because of quick processing pathways activated by dopamine. They are often quick thinking and tend to process their world orally, narrating their day. They are energized by conversation and typically use their communication skills to connect and reenergize. They tend to communicate openly and freely over a large range of topics (Laney, 2005).

Introverts, on the other hand, are more reserved in every aspect of their functioning. They ponder, process, and think about their feelings and thoughts before speaking. They are seldom impulsive with their words and rarely offer random commentaries on life. In fact, most introverts shy away from volunteering information about their thoughts and feelings. If you are interested in knowing what they think, then you are more likely to get information by asking them specific questions and allowing enough processing time for them to answer. They prefer to listen rather than speak. This isn't to say that introverts aren't good conversationalists. They can be, but only on topics of interest and with people they trust (Laney, 2005).

In addition to the differences in communication, extroverts and introverts also renew in different ways. As mentioned in Chapter 1, both groups rely on different aspects of their nervous system, with extroverts predominantly using the sympathetic nervous system, and introverts using the parasympathetic nervous system more regularly (Laney, 2002). It is not surprising, then, that the two groups are energized in different ways, with extroverts seeking connection and introverts seeking solitude. This difference in energy can often be why the two groups find it difficult to understand one another—what makes one happy and energized leaves the other feeling overwhelmed and agitated.

Figure 2 shows other ways that the two temperaments differ in terms of day-in, day-out functioning. As you can see, the two groups differ in almost every respect. Extroverts are more typically risk-takers, gain information through action, seldom hold back their emotions, are energized by people, and present in the same way publically and privately. Introverts are cautious and only take a risk once they understand the "rules" of the given situation. They gain information through thinking and introspection, and are intense in their emotions and tend to bottle them inside until they explode. They are fatigued by people and have two personas—one for the public and one for private.

Attributes	*Extroverts*	*Introverts*
Communication skills	Outgoing and talkative, somewhat impulsive	Reserved and quiet, prefers to listen rather than speak; can be good conversationalists in small groups.
Renewal pattern	Seeks stimulation externally through connections and action	Seeks stimulation internally through solitude and contemplation
Learning	Learns from the environment, through action; impulsive and willing to take risks.	Learns by watching and through internal contemplation and introspection; cautious.

Figure 2. Attributes of extroverts and introverts.

Knowing the differences between the two temperaments, both in terms of how the two biologically differ, as well as how those differences translate into attributes is only the beginning. Both temperaments have potential negative outcomes resulting from their unique attributes (see Figure 3). Extroverts can burn out from the overreliance on the sympathetic nervous system and the resultant desire for continuous stimulation. Introverts can become overly withdrawn when left alone for too long. Furthermore, they can become agitated when they have to spend too much time in social situations.

Both extroverts and introverts have things they can learn from their counterparts, behaviors they can emulate when needed. The extrovert can learn how to think more deliberately and how to relax. The introvert, in turn, can learn how to be more social and outgoing when the situation calls for it. The chart above shows interventions designed to address and mediate the potential negatives of each temperament.

In the next chapter, we will look more closely at the attributes of introversion, as well as why the Western culture favors the extrovert and what that means for our introverted children.

	Potential Problem	*Intervention*
Extroverts	*Overstimulation*: Burn-out resulting from an overreliance on the sympathetic nervous system *Understimulation*: Unable to focus, increased impulsivity	*Overstimulation*: Learn relaxation techniques; schedule short periods of calm and solitude into the day; learn self-monitoring techniques to regulate behavior and slow thinking down as needed *Understimulation*: Schedule periods of social connection and activity into the day; Learn self-monitoring techniques to increase focus; work for short periods of time, followed by activity
Introverts	*Overstimulation*: Increased agitation, short temper, emotional outbursts, excessive withdrawal *Understimulation*: Withdrawal and isolation	*Overstimulation*: Schedule periods of solitude into the day; learn calming strategies; seek solitude after long periods of social connection; set good boundaries on your time *Understimulation*: Schedule periods of activity into the day; make exercise a part of the day

Figure 3. The downside of temperament.

Class Notes: The Myths of Introversion

Ask educators for a synonym for introversion and they will typically come up with "shy" and "withdrawn." Rarely do they indicate the actual attributes of introversion, let alone their biological foundations. Part of the reason for this is due to the ways our Western culture has characterized introversion as being negative, something we will explore in greater depth in Chapter 3. This characterization has led to a number of ideas about introversion that are not rooted in research, a pathologizing of introversion connecting this temperament with everything from social anxiety and autism, to sensory integration problems and attention problems.

In truth, the disorders mentioned above can impact all temperaments. They are conditions that, despite some overlap, impact far more than the systems discussed with introversion, including all areas of a child's functioning.

What, then, is introversion? Sometimes the best way to understand the true attributes of introversion is to gain insight as to what it is not. As I mentioned earlier, our culture supports a negative view of introversion, one based on assumptions that distort the value of introversion in general (Laney, 2005).

One assumption comes from Freud's original ideas of introversion and involves the belief that introverts are more self-centered and self-absorbed than their extroverted counterparts. The truth is more complex. Introverts can often appear to be lost in their own thoughts. However, this is not a sign of some narcissism, just temperament. Introverted children are deep thinkers interested in deep feelings and beliefs. In this way, they can be strong contributors to groups if their need for a calm environment can be met or when the groups can be managed to maintain a small number.

A similar assumption is that introverts tend to shy away from friendships and prefer to be alone. As I mentioned above, introverts enjoy learning about other people. Friendships, especially ones with people who will volunteer information and take the lead in conversations, are important to introverts. It is true that introverts may "appear" to have less friends or prefer one or two very close relationships over a plethora of people to "hang out" with. But they still want the connection that a meaningful friendship brings.

As stated earlier, many people confuse shyness with introversion. In truth, a person of any temperament can appear "shy." Defined by the Merriam-Webster dictionary as someone who is easily frightened, hesitant in committing themselves, or avoidant of certain people or things, shyness crosses temperament and is often rooted in both the environment and experiences of the child. Although shyness does describe behaviors that many introverts demonstrate, extroverts are not immune from acting shy in specific situations. Consider the extroverted student who loves to be the "class clown" but avoids public speaking. He could be referred to as shy when it comes to that activity, despite being an extrovert. Or consider one of my earlier examples from my own life—how I overcame my reluctance to perform in front of others, but still continued to behave like an introvert in many other domains.

All in all, our culture continues to mislabel temperament with regard to introversion, coloring many of the associated behaviors in a negative or incorrect light. This mislabeling bleeds into the classroom, impacting the ability of our educational system to meet the needs of many of our introverted students. Educators teach in ways that enhance and appeal to extroversion, while minimizing activities that may be better suited for introverts. This is especially true in our era of peer-share and group-tasks education. We push our introverted children to speak more, think in specific ways, and limit creativity by reducing the "downtime" most creative endeavors require. And when our introverts are unsuccessful, we pathologize their temperament, mislabeling it again.

In the next chapter, we will examine some of the benefits of introversion to the classroom setting, focusing on the strengths of that temperament. Chapters 5–7 will focus even more closely on the ways in which introverted students learn.

ATTRIBUTES OF INTROVERSION Q&A

As illuminated throughout the chapter, extroverts and introverts behave in different ways as a result of their biological differences. No doubt, these differences have led to a few questions. Here are some of the questions that are regularly asked in my workshops and through letters and e-mails.

My son will take a lot of annoyance before responding, but when he does respond, there is often no warning—it's a 0–60, okay-to-major lash out. Is this typical, and how can we as parents combat this?

Yes, introverts do tend to bottle up their feelings, exploding when they can't take anything more. The result—explosive arguments and difficulties with both friendships and parent-child relationships. This happens because introverts struggle when it comes to openly talking about their feelings. They will answer specific questions, but only when they trust the person they are talking to and only when they have the words to pull from. This entire thing can be complicated further if you happen to have an intense child due to giftedness or other sensitivities.

Parents can help introverted children balance out this aspect of their temperament in a couple of ways: first, by creating a sense of trust with your child, and second, by teaching your child how to talk about his or her emotions at a young age. Helping him normalize his feelings goes a long way to assisting the introverted child in being willing to discuss his feelings.

There are many other tips that can help mediate the actual explosion or build-up of emotion that I will cover in the next few sections.

What are the different neurotransmitters impacting temperament, and how do they relate to the attributes of extroversion and introversion?

The two main neurotransmitters researched with reference to temperament are dopamine and acetylcholine. Dopamine, the main neurotransmitter responsible for reward-based learning in the brain and linked to activation of the sympathetic nervous system (such as "fight or flight"), is more widely utilized by extroverts. Use of this neurotransmitter is linked to the need of extroverts to seek others for renewal, as well as their quick thinking, willingness to take risks, and action-oriented behaviors.

Introverts tend to utilize acetylcholine as their preferred neurotransmitter. Acetylcholine is also involved in the autonomic nervous system functions, activating many parasympathetic nervous system functions (such as "rest and digest"). An introvert's use of acetylcholine is linked to her deep thinking and strong focusing abilities, as well as her seemingly slow response times when communicating and preference for calm and quiet environments.

It's important to remember that humans widely use many neurotransmitters throughout their daily functioning. But understanding which neurotransmitters are both preferred and function in rewarding ways to extroverts and introverts helps us to understand why and how temperament impacts daily functioning.

Is there a way to predict temperament based on a baby's over- or underreactions to the environment?

The works of Kagan and Snidman (2004) and Laney (2005) suggest that you can predict temperament based on a child's sensitivity to their environment, with highly sensitive babies being more likely introverted. That said, I would say that there are a lot of variables that influence how a child, especially a baby, interacts with his environment. Things like cognition, nutrition, prenatal influences, and familial environment are all highly influential to a baby's reactions to the environment, in addition to temperament. It would be somewhat impossible to regulate all of the variables to get a clean understanding of the ways in which each impacts functioning and responses. And I am not certain that is needed in order to understand an infant's responses and influence outcomes. More important, I think, is a global understanding of how all of the factors work together to shape and mold children.

Ultimately, babies want to feel safe within their environment. This involves knowing there is food available, having shelter, and most of all, having the presence of a caring caregiver to provide touch and security. If we focus first on these things, the influence of temperament, cognitive development, and other biologically framed attributes will become clear.

I find that as my introverted child ages, she is less introverted. Doesn't this contradict the idea that temperament is fixed and a matter of biology?

I love this question. It speaks to changes in our behavioral reaction to environmental situations, not our biology. Human beings are a true balance of nature and nurture. Although we cannot change our hardwiring, we can develop different patterns of responding to the world or new behaviors. The key is to take our basic hardwiring and look for ways to enhance our nature, not work against it. There are definite benefits to both introversion and extroversion. Working with our individual hardwiring is the key to developing our potential. Teaching our children to do the same is the key to developing theirs.

After seeing the differences between extroversion and introversion, I can really see that my students' temperaments have an impact on their learning. What advice do you have for educators on using this information in a classroom setting?

First, I think it is important to recognize the impact of temperament on learning and the classroom environment. Second, I think it is important to create somewhat neutral learning environments that neither overstimulate nor understimulate but provide a canvas upon which teaching and creation can occur. This means having a sensitive eye to things like loud, chaotic, visually overwhelming environments that can push an introvert into overload and overly quiet, sparse environments that make an extrovert cringe.

Once a neutral environment is created, an educator can look at creating safety within the environment, both in terms of taking academic risks, as well as allowing for well-balanced peer interactions. Including a variety of learning modalities and opportunities for mastery can also assist in creating places in which both extroverts and introverts can strive.

Above everything, I think it is important to remain open-minded, meeting your students where they are and bringing them to where you like them to be. This requires a clear understanding of your own biases and preferences and a willingness to remain open to your student despite these potential barriers. It can be a challenging thing, but staying neutral in terms of judgment is one of the best ways you can meet the needs of an ever-increasingly diverse student population.

In a Nutshell . . .

Big Ideas

- ❖ There are significant behavioral differences between extroverts and introverts.
- ❖ Introverts prefer to think and listen.
- ❖ Introverts seek solitude for renewal.
- ❖ Introverts need time to ponder questions before answering them.
- ❖ Introverts are deep thinkers and often bottle up their emotions until they explode.

❖ Both extroverts and introverts benefit from balancing their temperament.

Supplemental Pages
❖ Figure 2: Attributes of Extroverts and Introverts—page 21
❖ Figure 3: The Downside of Temperament—page 22

chapter 3

Soaring With Strengths

"I like being the way I am, being more reserved and quiet than most. I feel like I can think more clearly than many of my friends."—Blake, Age 17

The last two chapters outlined the biological and resultant behavioral differences between extroverts and introverts, highlighting both the positive and negative attributes. After going through them, it is clear that our Western cultural ideals lean more toward the extrovert. We set up our businesses and educational systems to function in groups, celebrating statements like "none of us are as good as all of us" and pushing "professional communities" as the axiom we should all embrace. We teach to the middle, insisting that in doing so we can pull everyone up to a certain level of achievement. We push aside creativity for more in-the-box, group thinking.

At the same time, our dichotomous Western culture also celebrates the individual. But only a particular type of individual—the outgoing, charismatic speaker that can charm his or her way through life with ease. We celebrate those who have physical prowess, take risks, and embrace life fully. We are drawn to those who know how to make small talk, have lots of friends, and are comfortable in the crowd.

Most of what is described above is well-suited for the extrovert. But where does that leave the introvert? Should the introvert try to be more extroverted? I would argue no, absolutely not. But before I get into that, I want to spend a little time talking about how our culture thinks about attributes typically associated with introversion.

The numbered descriptions in the worksheet on p. 31 are all things that I have heard in workshops, while coaching parents, and as part of my work as a school psychologist. As you consider each one, I want you to decide whether or not you agree with each statement or scenario.

I've done this exercise with hundreds of other educators, parents, and students over the past 15 years. It is clear as we work through each statement that our culture has done a disservice to our introverts, instilling a level of shame in those who demonstrate attributes of inversion. We tend to label deep thinkers as aloof and rude when they are young and odd when they are older. People who shy away from friends and social obligations will never make it to the top in the business world, and children who withdraw from others are labeled as socially disabled in some way.

The truth is, introversion is neither the narcissism described in Freud's day, nor is it something that needs to be "fixed" as it is often portrayed in our modern world.

In order to help introverts move past the shame of a culture that has not typically embraced them, it is important to first understand the positive aspects of introversion.

Many introverted children develop deep beliefs at an early age that guide them throughout their lives. This is related to their tendency to seek answers from within. As a result, they are often less dependent on external validation and more reliant on their inner strengths.

Additionally, many introverts are divergent thinkers, analyzing the world from a highly creative point of view. The solitude inherent with introversion is something typically connected to creativity (Cameron, 1992). This innate creativity sets the stage for the development of strong

WORKSHEET 3

Looking at My Beliefs (for Parents)

Directions: Read each of the 9 statements and determine if you agree or disagree with the statement.

	I agree	I disagree	I neither agree nor disagree
1. Introverted people are shy.			
2. Introverted people appear lonely and have few friends.			
3. Introverted people are more self-centered than others.			
4. Introverted people appear to get depressed more often.			
5. Introverted people have a hard time making friends.			
6. Introverted people need to learn social skills.			
7. Introverted people appear aloof.			
8. Introverted people are hindered by their shyness.			
9. Introverted people need to become more outgoing.			

Take a look at your answers and reflect on your beliefs. What are your feelings about introversion? Do you feel that being introverted is a disadvantage in our culture, something that needs to be changed? What are the drawbacks of introversion? The benefits? Use this information to help you understand your underlying feelings about temperament.

and diverse problem-solving skills, as well as the innovative thinking that is highly sought after in our modern world.

In addition to the internally driven thought process and creative thinking previously discussed, most introverts are born with a natural propensity toward well-developed emotional intelligence. Defined as the ability to acquire and apply emotional information, Daniel Goleman (1998) considered emotional intelligence to be at least as important as cognitive development. He postulated that emotional intelligence relied on the development of competency in five areas: Self-awareness, or the ability to recognize one's emotions; self-monitoring, or the ability to manage one's emotions from moment to moment; self-motivation, or the ability to act appropriately upon the emotions, which includes the development of self-discipline; empathy, or the ability to understand another person's emotions; and relationships, or the ability to develop intimate relationships with others (Goleman, 1998). These domains are all areas that come naturally to introverts, as they tend to reflect inward and process deep emotions and feelings internally.

As I mentioned above, the ability to form close relationships is one of the attributes of emotional intelligence. At first glance, it may seem that an introvert, with his tendency to shy away from people, may struggle in this domain. Actually, many introverts have a keen interest in the way the world works, including what motivates people. This gives an introvert the potential to develop strong connections with others, as his need to understand may drive him to delve more deeply into conversations.

Deep thinking, innovation, emotional intelligence, and the building of meaningful relationships—these are some of the most common gifts introverts have to share with the world. I will mention additional ones through the upcoming chapters. For a complete list of attributes, as well as the strengths and potential pitfalls in each area, refer to Figure 4: The Attributes of Introversion discussed in the Q&A section later in this chapter.

Class Notes: Enhancing the Positive Aspects of Introversion in Class

As mentioned earlier in the chapter, introverts clearly have many attributes that can translate to positive things in the classroom. Thinking deeply about information presented in classes, approaching tasks from a creative point of view, having empathy for others, developing intrinsic motivation, and demonstrating the capacity to develop deep, meaningful relationships are all attributes that an introvert brings to school. Unfortunately, not all classrooms support introverted students. Sometimes the setting is loud and overstimulating. Sometimes there is too much focus on group activities too early in the school year, preventing the introverted student from feeling comfortable. And sometimes the curriculum itself is focused on the type of mental processes that favor extroverted neurobiology.

Classrooms that enhance the positive aspects of introversion are places that feel calm, but not sterile. They allow some amount of freedom in how work is completed, do not demand that students constantly work in groups, and are a balanced mix of fast-paced and deeply engaging tasks. Teachers in these classrooms take time to get to know their students, provide a safe place in which taking academic risks is a natural part of learning, and understand that the introverted student often knows more than he or she appears to know.

Section three of this book, Introverted Kids at School, will cover many ways in which introverts learn, as well as specific strategies to enhance the many strengths of introversion. For now, it is important to focus on redefining introversion for yourself as an educator and embracing the many gifts introverts potentially bring to your classroom.

QUIET STRENGTH Q & A

We may live in a culture that supports and exalts extroversion as the ideal, but our introverts have a lot to offer the world as well. The following questions and answers address the strengths offered by introverts, even in a culture that is often noisy and chaotic.

What are some of the strengths and problems with introversion?

Throughout the chapter, I've explored the nuances of being introverted, looking at both the more typical strengths and some of the challenges. Figure 4 is a list that summarizes some the attributes of introversion, including the negative and positive aspects of each one.

As you can see in Figure 4, introverts bring a lot of positives to light. The ability to think creatively, pursue interests with passion, and gain a deep meaning out of life are all attributes that can lead to an intense level of satisfaction with life when nurtured. This is what introverts have to offer when they are allowed to develop their skills to their fullest.

Is there anything wrong with being an introvert?

This is sort of like asking if there is anything wrong with being blonde. Or if there is anything wrong with having difficulty keeping things organized. It simply is what it is—it is how a person is hardwired. That said, there are some aspects of introversion that can be more problematic than others. For example, having difficulties interacting with peers, something that can be typical in younger introverts, can be a problem in a school setting in which there are a lot of group activities or limited places for the introvert to get away from the crowd at lunch. Likewise, some introverts can struggle with too much visual, auditory, or emotional input, resulting in some problem behaviors. This can be a problem in very public places like the mall or amusement parks. These difficulties need not prevent the introvert from interacting with the world, however. The upcoming chapters will focus on several strategies that can help introverted children

Strengths	Potential Problems
Deep thinkers	May overthink simple things
Highly creative and innovative	Takes a long time to complete tasks
Works well independently	May struggle with collaboration
Curious	May resist transitioning to new things
Thinks before taking action	Overly cautious
Builds deep connections and relationships	May struggle to form friendships initially

Figure 4. The attributes of introversion.

and their parents learn to cope with some of the difficulties introverts may face.

What advice can you give introverts to capitalize on their strengths?

I think the most important thing is for the introvert to gain awareness of how her introversion impacts her, both positively and negatively, as well as developing coping strategies for the aspects of introversion that are a problem. The worksheet on page 36 will assist the introverted child and his or her parents in identifying some of the impacts, positive and negative, of introversion.

Once this information is ascertained, appropriate strategies are found in the later chapters of this book that can be helpful in teaching introverts how to capitalize on their many strengths.

What is the difference between introversion and shyness?

This is probably the most frequent question I am asked on the topic of temperament. As I stated earlier in the book, shyness refers to behaviors including being withdrawn, suspicious, timid, or reluctant. It can be a situation-specific behavior or something that is exhibited in multiple settings. And, unlike introversion, it is something that is highly dependent on context and environment.

Introversion, on the other hand, is not dependent on environmental factors. Introverts are not wary or suspicious by definition, but can behave in that way if the environment is new to them. Furthermore,

WORKSHEET 4

The Positive Aspects of My Introversion

Directions: Read the attribute and decide if it is true for you and how you feel about it. Be sure to indicate those things that present a problem or a concern for you:

Attribute	This Is True for Me. (Y/N)	My Feelings About This:
Deep thinker		
Highly creative and innovative		
Works well independently		
Curious		
Thinks before taking action		
Builds deep connections and relationships		
May overthink simple things		
Takes a long time to complete tasks		
May struggle with collaboration		
May resist transitioning to new things		
Overly cautious		
May struggle to form friendships initially		

many shy individuals may be reluctant to interact socially, while introverts may enjoy social connections, but become fatigued by too many of them.

For me, the easiest way to remember the difference is to remember that shyness is a behavior that can be exhibited by both introverts and extroverts and is generally influenced by the person's reactions to his or her environment.

As an educator, I see my introverted children struggling related to the attributes you've described. How can I help them to see some of their difficulties as potential strengths?

This is a great question. Like the earlier question, focusing on how introversion impacts a student in both positive and negative ways is a great first step in working with the introverted student. Use Worksheet 4 on page 36 with the introverted student and assist the student in determining what introversion means to her. Then, help the child reframe the aspects of temperament she has identified as being problematic in a new, positive light. For example, if the student has identified her reluctance to participate in a group as a source of distress, help her both reframe the attribute as the ability to function well independently and develop a strategy to deal with working in a group. Assisting the student in this way will have her embracing her unique strengths in no time.

In a Nutshell . . .

Big Ideas

- ❖ Introverts have positive qualities or gifts.
- ❖ The Western cultural often misunderstands the attributes of introversion, labeling it with terms including narcissism, being rude, and being aloof.
- ❖ Introverts are deep thinkers and enjoy learning new things.
- ❖ Introverts have a natural tendency to think in creative and innovative ways.

❖ Introverts have a natural ability to develop strong emotional intelligence related to the depths of their internal thought processes.

❖ Introverts are capable of developing deep and meaningful relationships with others.

Supplemental Pages

chapter 4

In Their Own Words

A Matter of Temperament

Ten years ago, I started adding the topic of temperament to my giftedness-related workshops. Every time the workshop was held, a member of the audience would express some form of an "aha" moment, a sudden insight about how introversion or extroversion applied to his or her household.

On one particular night, while setting up for the workshop, one of my frequent participants arrived early. She wanted to share some of her recent experiences with temperament at home and how her change in understanding of introversion and extroversion positively impacted her home. Her story was followed by two others, each from different participants.

The story below is a combination of those three stories that were shared. The names have all been changed, as well as some of the identifying details. But the point of the story—the impact of understanding temperament and its impact on the household functioning—remains the same.

I always thought I understood my husband and my children. After all, I had been a wife for more than 14 years, and a mother for 12. Turns out, I didn't know as much as I thought I did.

Our household is typical of most in my middle-class suburban community. My husband and I both work full time. He is in middle management for a local company, working reasonable hours for reasonable pay. I work at a local school, teaching English literature to high school students.

We have three children—a 5-year-old boy, a 10 year-old girl, and an 11 year-old girl. Like most of the families in my neighborhood, we spend a little too much money, work a little too long in our jobs, and spend too little time with our children.

Most nights, I am too exhausted to deal with the kids and my husband. I work late grading papers and often find myself wanting to hide the minute I get home. Unfortunately, my husband and kids usually have different plans.

Every night the kids want to tell me all about their day, sparing me none of the details. They like it when I help with homework, even though they don't "need" my help. I think they just like me to be close.

In truth, I love spending time with them—I love hearing about their days and seeing their homework. But, after spending all day teaching and all afternoon grading, I am completely spent when I get home.

At night, my husband usually wants to tell me about his business adventures. We used to spend a lot of time sharing the exploits of the day with each other. Now, even though I love hearing about his life, I am tired and want to just go to sleep.

Part of me wants to hide and pretend I'm alone in the evenings. But that idea just makes me feel guilty. I mean, what mother doesn't want her children and her husband to share their days with her? So I just stuff back the random frustration I feel and stay focused on being a good mom and wife.

Until I blow up for no reason—something that is happening a little too often.

At least it was, before I learned about temperament.

It happened during a workshop about gifted children. The presenter introduced the ideas of extroversion and introversion to the audience, stating that extroverts liked to "renew" at the end of the day by talking and connecting socially, whereas introverts needed solitude in order to renew. The more the presenter talked about these two forms of temperament, the more I began to think that a lot of my pointless frustration at home was related to this.

I went home and did my own research, discovering that extroversion and introversion really was about how a person renews emotionally. I began to think that my problem at home was that I was introverted while the other members of my household were not. The more I observed my children and husband, the more I started to believe that differences in temperament explained everything.

After about a month of pondering and stewing on this, I decided to go back to the presenter from the workshop and ask her opinion. She and I met for coffee the next week. I asked her about the specific characteristics of introversion. She explained that introverts can become agitated around extroverts, especially if they are already tired from spending a lot of time around other people. She went on to use the example of a teacher she knew who was introverted and how the nature of a teacher's job was exhausting to her friend—enjoyable, but exhausting.

Yes. That was it. The job was exhausting. I, too, felt "spent" after a day at work. I needed downtime in order to renew before having to connect with my family.

After about an hour of talking, I felt like I had finally figured out my personal source of discomfort at home. I spoke with my husband, explaining my introversion tendencies. Together, we came up with ways to reorganize the evenings, allowing me some "alone" time before getting home.

Within a week, I noticed a significant difference in how I interacted with my children and my husband. No longer apprehensive when I got home, I discovered that I could enjoy spending time with my children and husband again. I just needed to make sure that I remembered to give myself ample opportunities for solitary renewal.

Understanding my temperament, as well as the temperament of my children and husband, was one of the most important and influential things I have ever learned. By giving each of us what we need according to our temperament, we have managed to create a household that works for all of us.

This story is just one example of how understanding temperament can influence the ways a parent can structure the environment to reduce the negative things that can occur when anyone—parent or child— becomes emotionally exhausted and unable to adequately renew. In my own household, we are three introverts and one extrovert. Understanding how the needs of my extroverted daughter were not getting met in the world of introversion created at home, as well as understanding why her energy so often conflicted with my own was a godsend. It enabled me to create time at the end of my day to renew *before* going home, in order to be able to connect with her and allow her to tell me about her day without reacting to the frenetic qualities of her energy.

The following section will illustrate some specific ways families can come to terms with the diverse needs of multitemperament households, as well as the enrichment that comes from having both introverts and extroverts in the house.

part II

Introverted Kids at Home

Parents are charged with the responsibility of preparing their children for adulthood. When you are the parent of an introverted child, this responsibility can be challenging. As I previously mentioned, our world is geared for extroverts. But what happens to introverts? What about their unique strengths and gifts? How do those fit into our world? And how do you enhance your child's strengths in a world that may not always express tolerance for his or her temperament?

The next chapters look at the job of parenting introverted children, examining the environments in which introverts thrive, as well as meeting the needs of both extroverts and introverts in the home and working with extended support systems.

As you begin to take stock of your home life, it is important to examine the truth of your current home environment as well as the things that are working and those that may need adjustment. Take a moment to complete the questionnaire on page 44 before moving into the next chapters.

QUESTIONNAIRE 2

Ideas About Parenting Introverts

1. I know my temperament and the temperament of the members of the household.

    ❑ *True*   ❑ *False*

2. I think temperament matters when it comes to parenting my children.

    ❑ *True*   ❑ *False*

3. The biggest challenges I have faced parenting my introverted children are . . . (*complete the sentence*).

4. I think my household has been previously more geared toward one temperament or another.

    ❑ *True*   ❑ *False*

5. My children have varied temperaments (introversion and extroversion).

    ❑ *True*   ❑ *False*

6. If I answered "true" above, I think the biggest difficulties in parenting a split temperament household has been . . . (*complete the sentence*).

Once you are finished, take a moment to reflect on your answers and consider the following questions: What are my main goals for this section of the book? What answers am I hoping to find? Take a moment to write down your thoughts regarding parenting introverts and the home environment as it relates to introverts.

chapter 5

Setting the Foundation

"My parents don't really understand me. They want me to have a ton of friends. But I am happy just the way I am."—Olivia, Age 12

Effective parenting begins with both an understanding of the child, as well as an understanding of how the household environment impacts the behavioral reactions of children. The first section of the book focused on explaining the basic attributes of temperament, as well as how to determine which members of your household are introverted. This section focuses on parenting strategies used with introverts. And the best place to start this conversation is with parenting ideas that work particularly well with introversion, ideas that will establish a strong foundation of support for the introvert.

Introverted children function best in predictable environments that are calm, organized, and allow for periods of rest. This is not always easy to find with today's busy and somewhat chaotic lifestyle.

Fortunately, the same conditions that assist the introverted child also form the foundations of effective parenting. Attributes including clear expectations regarding behavior, clearly defined consequences, boundaries, predictable reactions from parents, and opportunities for involvement in the household through chores and input regarding rules and consequences all contribute to laying a strong foundation for the introverted child.

Before I discuss the specific qualities of each of these attributes, take a moment and complete the household inventory worksheet on page 47. This will help you get a handle on the specifics of your household.

Most parents see the value in clear expectations and consequences for behavior. Ensuring that every member of the household understands the rules and consequences for both good and not-so-good behavior will create the predictability that introverts respond well to. It will also help the introverted child understand just what is expected of her with regard to chores and other responsibilities, as well as behavior. This can help to ensure compliance most of the time.

It is important to note that most introverts will comply with family expectations when they are not overextended. However, once they become overwhelmed, the introverted child will get particularly stubborn, refusing to comply with many of the most simple and basic of rules. This situation can be made worse when parental reactions are harsh, demanding compliance with little time allotted to the child to process the request and calm down.

In addition to clearly understanding the rules and expectations of the household, introverted children function best with predictable routines. Having a bedtime routine, as well as homework and morning routines, can do a lot for the introverted child in terms of creating a safe and nurturing environment. Preparing the child for changes to the routine whenever possible can also extend that feeling of safety through times of potential turmoil.

When rules and expectations are clear, and routines are in place, children will often strive to please their parents. But what happens when they don't? Are there methods of discipline that are more effective than others?

Just as it is important to have clear expectations, it is equally important to have clear consequences for behavior. For example, if the expec-

WORKSHEET 5

My Household Foundation

Directions: Read each statement as it relates to your household and decide if you agree or disagree with the statement. For additional benefit, allow each family member to complete a worksheet.

	I agree	I disagree	I neither agree nor disagree
1. Each person in the household knows the expectations or rules.			
2. The rules have meaning to the members of the household.			
3. Each household member knows the consequences for breaking a rule.			
4. Consequences are consistently applied.			
5. Every household member knows his or her role in the family structure.			
6. Each member of the household respects the boundaries of the others.			
7. Parents are predictable and consistent in their reactions to the children.			
8. Household members have chores and know what the chores are.			
9. Children participate in some of the decisions in the household.			
10. Every member of the household has opportunities to contribute to the running of the household.			

Looking through the worksheet, what do you notice? Is there disagreement between any of the household members? Are there areas that need clarification?

tation is that their beds are made before the children leave for school, there should be a consequence for both compliance and noncompliance. Many times there are natural consequences to behavior. But when these are too distant or lack sufficient motivation to manage the behavior, it is important to have consequences in place and discuss them with the children. Using the bed-making example above, a consequence for compliance could be earning time to spend on a preferred activity, while lack of compliance could mean not earning the time.

For the most part, better compliance is obtained when the focus of discipline is positive in nature. This type of discipline puts the child in charge of the consequence in that the child's behavior determines the response, just as it does in life. It removes the emotional hook and power struggle that can often happen with discipline.

This type of positive discipline is particularly effective with introverted children because it keeps the child from becoming overwhelmed by the emotional drama that can ensue when consequences are punitive. Furthermore, it allows for breathing room, planned reactions, and opportunities to cool down for both the parent and the child. All of these work in favor with the temperament of the introvert.

Behavioral difficulties happen with any child from time to time. These difficulties are often a response to feeling overwhelmed with the environment. They can be reduced in introverted children by taking a calm and unemotional approach to correcting behavior. As I mentioned earlier in the chapter, introverts don't respond well to demands for compliance, especially when they are accompanied by yelling, screaming, or a harsh tone of voice. They often become rigid, stubborn, and explosive. Remembering that behavioral difficulties are a normal part of growing up can help parents keep their cool. Furthermore, reframing the behavior as a teachable moment is a great way to stay focused on positive discipline. The tip sheet on page 49 contains a series of questions you can ask yourself to determine if your methods of discipline are positive in nature.

Another factor involved in the establishment of a strong household foundation for introverts is the establishment and maintenance of clear boundaries between all household members. This means establishing the parents as parents and the children as children.

TIP SHEET 1

Positive Discipline

Ask yourself the following questions related to discipline:

❖ What is my current method of discipline?

❖ Keeping in mind your current discipline strategy, answer the following questions:

   o Will this teach my child better decision-making skills?

   o Does the discipline change the misbehavior?

   o Does this reduce the need for more discipline?

   o Am I angry when I discipline my children?

   o Am I impulsive with regard to discipline?

   o What is my goal with regard to discipline?

Positive discipline focuses on teaching or reteaching skills and not punitive consequences. Take time to check your use of discipline whenever you feel it is losing its effectiveness.

The parents' role in the family structure involves establishing rules and consequences, supporting healthy decision making for all household members, and coaching the children toward the development of strong resiliency and good social skills. Clear boundaries allow the children to remain children within the family structure, something important in our current culture that tends to rush children into adult roles before they are ready from an emotional standpoint. Introverts, in particular, benefit from the predictability of boundaries in the same way that they benefit from clear family structure.

The establishment of clear boundaries is not limited to the roles of parent and child; it also involves boundaries between parents and between siblings. With parents, it is important for each parent to allow the other to form his or her own relationship with the children. Maintaining appropriate boundaries such as not interfering when one parent is disciplining the children or when one parent is coaching behavior is a great way to help children respect both parents equally. When there is disagreement between the parents, it should be discussed outside of the earshot of the children.

With siblings, it is important that the introverted child be allowed personal space, either by having a part of a room that he can call his own or by having a separate room. Having this space enables the introverted child to create a "mini-retreat" that will serve as a sanctuary when he needs to renew.

In addition to establishing personal space, it is important for introverted children to feel like they have privacy. This means teaching the other household members to respect the "alone time" of the child, by remembering to knock before entering a room or respecting a specific time set aside as "quiet time." Doing this gives the introverted child much-needed space and time for a respite from the busyness of the day or from extroverted family members. The tip sheet on page 51 provides a few questions you and your children can use as reminders when establishing appropriate boundaries.

I mentioned earlier that introverted children function best when their environment is somewhat predictable. This extends beyond household routines and expectations to the reactions of the parents themselves. The more stable and predictable the reaction from each parent, the more the introverted child is able to adapt to the situation and feel safe within the environment.

Environments in which parents are consistently firm, but calm, when dealing with behavior tend to yield the most positive results with introverted children. Environments in which parental reaction appears random and chaotic often lead to feelings of anxiety in children. And introverted children do not react well to even small amounts of stress, often resulting in behavior that is either withdrawn or rigid and explosive.

But how can parents stay calm and collected all of the time? The answer is, they can't, and they should not be expected to be calm 24/7. Parents are first and foremost human. As such, they are subject to emotional highs and lows and behavioral ups and downs—just like everyone else.

The key to reacting in a stable, calm manner most of the time is to know your "hot-button" issues—those issues that typically elicit strong, sometimes overwhelming, emotional responses. Now, I know we'd like

TIP SHEET 2
Boundary Reminders

❖ What is your role in the relationship?
❖ Are you respecting the boundaries of those around you?
❖ Are they respecting your boundaries?
❖ Do you know what to do if your boundaries are being ignored?

to think that we don't have too many of those. And maybe that is true for you when you are well-rested and calm. But in today's world, how often does that happen? We spend much of our day tired and emotionally drained. And if you are like many parents, you do not consistently take care of yourself. At these times, those "hot-button" issues can be a significant trigger, and when they are pushed, watch out!

Managing your own behavioral response may take some effort, especially during times of stress. But you cannot expect your child to manage her emotions when you are unable to manage your own. The tip sheet on page 52 lists a few self-reflection questions you can use to help get your reactions under control. These are also tips you can use with your children as they learn to manage their own reactions.

As I mentioned in previous chapters, introverts tend to develop connections at a deep level. Creating a household foundation that fosters a sense of community enhances the introverted child's natural ability to develop relationships. One way to accomplish this is by involving the child in the running of the household through chores and input on some decisions (like where to take a vacation or what do to on a family game night).

Chores are important for children for a number of reasons. Having responsibility for things like keeping their bedrooms clean, helping with meal preparations and clean-up, and taking care of the family pet are all activities that teach both respect for one's things and discipline. Furthermore, chores are a vehicle that can reinforce the child's involvement in the running of the household.

TIP SHEET 3

Managing My Reactions

❖ Am I paying attention to my emotional reaction to my children?

❖ Have I become emotionally "hooked" by my child?

❖ Am I detached from the drama?

❖ Am I staying focused on outcomes?

❖ Can I remain calm or do I need to take a break?

Another way in which children can build a connection to the household unit is through family meetings. More than a time for parents to share information, family meetings can provide a forum for children to speak out and share their thoughts regarding important issues in the family. It is important to note that such meetings may be difficult for the introverted child at first. Uncomfortable with any form of confrontation or being expected to respond quickly to questions, many introverted children will be reluctant to speak out on issues. However, by making meetings a normal part of the family's routine, as well as allowing for multiple ways to participate, the introverted child will learn how to utilize this type of vehicle as a means to connect and participate in family decisions.

No chapter covering parenting and introverts is complete without discussion of some of the hard conversations parents need to have with their children. We live in a world filled with potential risks for our children. Sex and drug and alcohol use are all areas teens are confronted with well before they enter high school. How can parents best address some of these things, especially when introverted children shy away from such intense levels of conversation? The answer lies in the development of strong communication skills long before the need for these types of conversations arises. Introverted children, as discussed in previous chapters, are deep thinkers capable of making deep connections. As such, they are seldom impulsive in their decision making. This will work in favor of reduced risky behaviors. But it does not render the introverted child immune to the risks—in fact, his reluctance to be confrontational could place him in bigger levels of risk.

Establish a plan with your children with regard to risky behaviors. Make certain your children understand your expectations and the rules governing such behaviors. Work together on a game plan that addresses what to do if and when they find themselves in the middle of high-risk situations. Talk often and regularly about these topics, making certain your children know that you are comfortable talking with them. At the same time, don't mandate that they talk with you. Remember that introverts may feel excessively awkward with such conversations and may withdraw. Do not mistake this for disinterest. Continue letting them know your thoughts and opinions as situations arise.

I've presented several ways to create a strong family foundation in the preceding pages. The next chapters cover additional areas in which parents are positioned to make a significant impact—building resiliency and responding to stress and anxiety in a healthy manner. But before we get to that, let's look at the classroom environment and a little parenting Q&A.

Class Notes: Setting the Expectation in Light of Temperament

Classrooms are often microcosms of our society. As such, a teacher can expect to have extroverts and introverts at about a 2-1 ratio. Establishing effective classrooms with mixed temperaments can have its challenges, as each temperament thrives with its own set of conditions. Add things like language and cultural differences, learning differences, and gender differences, and it is not surprising that many teachers often feel like they are just trying to keep up with the demands, let alone establish an environment that enhances and optimizes learning.

Setting expectations in the diverse classroom is difficult, to be certain. But understanding how the different temperaments function can give insight as to how to establish expectation baselines for individual children.

Extroverts often thrive in classrooms that are alive with activity and sensory input. They enjoy the dynamics of collaboration, often have good short-term and rote memory skills and need stimulation in order to engage in learning. The current teaching principles that emphasize group dynamics, quick processing, and mastery of facts are in direct alignment with how the majority of extroverts function in class.

Introverts, on the other hand, perform best when creativity and deep thinking is emphasized. They benefit from learning depth, not breadth. They are often divergent thinkers and thrive when given ample time to both process and demonstrate their knowledge. They do not benefit from the quick quiz format that exists in many of today's classrooms. Furthermore, they do not respond well to public chastisement or confrontational methods of classroom discipline.

Given the differences, how can a teacher establish expectations for both sets of temperaments? The key, I believe, lies in how the classroom activities are structured. Balancing activities between group and individual is essential. Furthermore, allowing for deeper levels of study on topics and diversity within assignments allows both temperaments to prosper in the educational setting.

Establishing classroom expectations that focus on achieving personal success balanced with small-group activities, as well as allowing for divergent thinking, creative problem solving, and nontraditional learning are all ways that enhance both temperaments. Finally, ensuring that the classroom is safe from bullying in all its forms, particularly the subtle relational aggression that can easily occur without teacher awareness, allows all children to feel safe and be more willing to take academic risks.

PARENTING INTROVERTS Q&A

Meeting the needs of the introverted child can be difficult, especially if one or both of the parents are extroverts. In the parenting classes I've conducted over the past decade, questions often arise about how to establish a strong foundation to help enhance the introvert. Couched in phrases like "help my introvert come out of her shell" and "How can I make him more social?", the questions don't always focus on strengthening the many skills of the introvert.

Below you'll find some of the more typical questions I've received over the years, along with some specific information designed to promote the strengths of introversion, as well as minimize some of the problems.

Is there such a thing as an "ideal" home environment for an introvert?

It would be great if there was a cookbook answer for things, wouldn't it? But, sadly, there is no one-size-fits-all answer for this. There are, however, some things that work best for introverted children. First, introverted children function best in a household that is calm, somewhat free from clutter, and organized. They thrive when things are predictable and routine. Introverted children also function best when given their own space—a bedroom or a specific section in a shared bedroom—that they can decorate as they choose. The more autonomy they have over that space, the better. They need a comfortable place where they can unwind and shut the world away, especially if they are involved in a number of social activities or around a lot of people for long periods of time.

A few other environmental things that can help the introverted child include: predictable routines around bedtime, mornings, homework, etc.; opportunities for solitude; reduced pressure when she is overextended; and meal options that are balanced and have protein and regular intervals. All of these things can help restore an introvert and allow her to function at her best.

What is the most effective way to discipline/reprimand an introverted child?

Like all children, introverts respond best to positive behavioral strategies that focus on seeing behavior problems as opportunities to teach or reteach the introverted child a specific skill he is lacking. For example, introverted children often shut down when pushed too hard. This behavior can be mistaken for being rude or unmotivated. In reality, the behavior is both a response to being overwhelmed with environmental demands and an indicator that the child may lack the essential social skill of being able to ask for a break or help. If a parent responds simply by getting angry and punishing the child, the opportunity to teach the missing skill is lost and the child will likely engage in the behavior again at some point. Instead, the parent should focus on teaching the missing skill, as well as setting clear boundaries for behavior.

This is not to say that there should be no consequence for the problem behaviors. Life does not function that way. But the consequence should be administered with an understanding of the underlying function or reason for the behavior and should be congruent with the problem behavior.

Using the example above, I would advise taking a three-step response to the behavior. First, prompt the child to ask for a break or help by saying something like "it seems like maybe you need to take a break." If the child reacts by taking a break, praise her actions when she reengages. Focus on teaching the missing skill after the problem has passed.

Sometimes the child will not respond appropriately to the prompt. He or she may yell in response or speak in a disrespectful tone. At that point, I would advise that "time away" be given to the child. What the child—and probably the parent—needs is a break to calm down and decompress. Time away can provide that, as well as some of the other strategies already mentioned in the chapter. After the break, a natural consequence could be having to apologize. If the inappropriate verbal outburst was particularly bad, a consequence could also be the loss of a privilege for a short period of time. It is just important to remember that misbehavior is an opportunity for the child to learn a skill. It should not turn into a power struggle, especially with introverts.

What are some strategies you can use to get your introverted children to share news about their day?

As I mentioned earlier in the chapter, we parents love trying to get our introverted children to talk at the most inopportune times, like immediately after school or after a large social gathering. This is one of the worst times to try to get the introverted child to speak. He likely needs downtime to process the day a bit before we insist on news.

Once the timing of when to ask questions about the day is solved, there are a few things you can do to help your child open up. First, stay away from yes or no questions. If given a chance, an introverted child will answer the questions with "no" or "I don't know." Also, give plenty of time for the child to answer each question. Finally, ask clarifying ques-

TIP SHEET 4

Getting My Introverted Child to Open Up

❖ Allow decompression time after school or social activities before initiating conversations.
❖ Be careful of yes/no questions.
❖ Allow for processing time.
❖ Don't fire off too many questions at once.
❖ Allow your child the space and choice not to answer.
❖ Be aware of other opportunities to communicate, such as during a car ride or while doing the dishes. Many introverts are more likely to open up when the pressure to talk is reduced.

tions when your child answers, to assist in the conversation. The tip sheet on page 57 can serve as a reminder when helping your child communicate with you.

Help! One of my children is an extrovert and the other two are introverts. Do you have any tips for smoothing out the battles that ensue with a mixed-temperament household?

Mixed temperaments is something that almost all multichild households face. The key in managing this is to both set up an environment that is balanced between meeting the needs of the introvert (calm and organized) and meeting the needs of the extrovert (vibrant and social), and allowing all household members to soar with their strengths. For the introvert, this may mean having clear boundaries that allow the introvert downtime, away from the extroverts of the house. For the extrovert, it may mean scheduling some social time during the day and focusing on building connections.

In either case, the more all household members can begin to understand both their own temperament nuances and those of the other household members, the better. Take a moment and revisit the Understanding My Child's Temperament worksheet in Chapter 1 (see page 10) to remember what the temperaments currently are in your home. The key to balance starts with this information.

My classroom is definitely a mixed temperament environment. What can I do to help ensure the comfort of my introverted students?

Introverts need a calming environment for learning, something I discuss in great length in Section III. A calming environment can be achieved through similar strategies as those discussed earlier for the home. Predictable routines, clear expectations, and an authoritarian approach to teaching are all things that will enable an introvert to find comfort in the classroom setting. Other things that can comfort an introvert include a balance between group and individual activities, flexibility regarding oral projects, and time to process information. These strategies will help bring out the best in the introverted child.

In a Nutshell . . .

Big Ideas

- ❖ Introverts thrive in environments that are calm and organized.
- ❖ Introverts respond best when expectations are clear, boundaries are specific, and there are opportunities to connect to the family unit.
- ❖ Introverts need personal space and personal time in order to renew.
- ❖ Behavioral difficulties can arise when the introverted child becomes overwhelmed.
- ❖ Introverted children respond best to positive discipline, predictable routines, and authoritative parenting styles.

Supplemental Pages

- ❖ Worksheet 5: My Household Foundation—page 47
- ❖ Tip Sheet 1: Positive Discipline—page 49
- ❖ Tip Sheet 2: Boundary Reminders—page 51

- ❖ Tip Sheet 3: Managing My Reactions—page 52
- ❖ Tip Sheet 4: Getting My Introverted Child to Open Up—page 57

chapter 6

Nurturing Resiliency

"I am tired of feeling like I don't quite fit in, tired of being ashamed of how shy I am in every situation."—Sun, Age 13

Resiliency, defined by the Merriam-Webster Dictionary as the ability to recover or adjust to change, is a necessary tool in today's ever-changing world. Parents serve as a child's first coach in this vital area and make the difference between the child developing a strong level of resiliency or being vulnerable to life's chaotic whims with few emotional resources to draw on for support.

Researchers have determined three predominant attributes to resiliency—the development of a strong sense of autonomy or mastery over one's environment, the ability to connect deeply with others and find support and comfort in that connection, and the ability to manage one's emotional reactivity to life's situations—and several subdomains within the attributes that contribute to the framework of resiliency

(Prince-Embury, 2005). All of these aspects woven together can provide children with a layer of protection against the hardships of life. Over the next several pages, I will examine the various attributes, pointing out ways that introverted children may be at risk, as well as providing strategies for parents to reduce the risk factors and nurture resiliency.

As mentioned above, developing a strong sense of autonomy over your environment is one of the cornerstone factors for the development of resiliency. Introverted children, who seldom feel control over the environments at home and at school, can struggle in this area as they grow and develop. Taking a closer look at the development of autonomy can provide some insight as to why introverted children may struggle, as well as point the way to strategies parents can use to negate the potential negative impacts.

Optimism, or the ability to see the positives in life, factors greatly in the development of autonomy over one's environment. Furthermore, the ability to adapt to life's curveballs without becoming overwhelmed is another important aspect in learning to master your environment. Both of these factors can be somewhat problematic for introverted children. As the introverted child becomes overwhelmed with environmental demands, she gets stuck. Changes in routine will often result in stubbornness as a way for the introverted child to establish control whenever she feels her life spiraling out of control. The child may dig in her heels, refuse to accept any form of help, and adapt a pessimistic point of view as life's demands begin to overwhelm her temperament. Eventually, if the child is not coached how to regain some autonomy over the situation, an explosion will ensue, all because the child got "stuck."

So what is a parent to do? How can you help your child prevent the rigidity and stubbornness that often comes when his mastery over the environment is threatened?

I think the answer is two-fold. First, it is important to allow the child as much control as is appropriate over the situation. The tip sheet on page 63 can help you know what questions to ask yourself as you determine how much choice or control to give the child.

The second step is teaching children how to recognize what aspects of life are within their control and which things are not, as well as what to do about it all. In doing this, introverted children learn the art of

TIP SHEET 5
Sharing Control

The following self-reflection questions can help when determining how much autonomy to give your child:

* ❖ Will my child be safe with either choice?
* ❖ Is my child able to make this decision?
* ❖ What is the downside to either decision?
* ❖ Will the opportunity for choice hinder my child's development in some way?

discernment, a skill that will forever enhance their ability to not only develop a sense of mastery over their world, but also learn how to let go of things outside their sphere of control. It is a skill that will help them learn to regulate their moods and adapt to a world that will not always understand their introverted ways.

To learn discernment, I use a technique I originally developed in my work with gifted children, called the Hula Hoop technique. The tip sheet on page 64 outlines the technique and how to teach it to your children. Use this whenever your introvert is getting stuck and rigid. It may help to calm down the rigidity before it gets too far out of hand.

Self-efficacy, or the belief that you can perform successfully in a given situation, is one of the last factors influencing autonomy. Believing that you are able to navigate life's ups and downs requires both good problem-solving skills and the ability to seek help when needed. Introverted children are often innovative problem solvers. Using their natural tendency to seek complex connections, they are often able to navigate most problems when they are afforded enough contemplation time. The problem comes when they are expected to work more quickly than is comfortable or when they need to ask for help. These two situations can be challenging for the introverted child and can negatively influence the overall development of strong self-efficacy skills. Parents can help to support introverted children by encouraging children to ask for help, teaching a few "survival" extroversion skills, and refining their problem-solving

---

TIP SHEET 6

The Hula Hoop Technique

❖ Imagine there is a hula hoop or some other circle on the ground.
❖ Step into the middle of it.
❖ Everything *outside* of the circle is outside of your control. This includes friends, family, school . . . everything. Except you!
❖ Everything *inside* of the circle you have 100% control over, including your thoughts, feelings, beliefs, and actions.

The next time something upsets you, use this technique and decide whether or not it is something you can control. If it is, great! You can change it to change how you feel. But if it is not, then you need to let it go and move forward.

---

skills. We will be addressing each of these in the upcoming chapters. For now, focus on teaching discernment and adaptability as effective ways to nurture the development of autonomy.

Before I move on to the other aspects of resiliency, I want to point out one of the strongest attributes of introversion is related to the development of an internal sense of mastery over one's environment. Feeling a sense of mastery requires belief in your ability to have some control over the world around you. Introverts, by nature, do not look outward for confirmation or validation. They rely on their inner strengths and dialogues as a measure of their ability to master their feelings and their environment. This attribute can be coached into a significant strength as introverted children begin to use that natural tendency for discernment toward the development of a strong self-efficacy.

Building supportive connections is another major aspect of resiliency. Although I will be discussing the social aspects of introversion, I wanted to take a moment now to discuss it as it relates to resiliency. Built on the factors of acceptance, comfort, and support, building connections can be both a challenge and a potential strength for introverted children.

Introverted children are not shy by definition. They are keenly interested in people, often wanting to get to know them at a deep level. However, they are not always comfortable around people, especially larger groups. In these situations, the introvert is often overwhelmed, resulting in withdrawal.

Acceptance is another thing that can impact the building of supportive connections. If the introverted child has been accepted by parents and siblings, as well as at school, then he is more likely to develop strength with regard to connections and resiliency. However, if the child has been rejected or misunderstood related to his introversion, the opposite may occur and the child will again become overwhelmed and withdrawn.

Parents can help introverted children develop strong and supportive connections by providing a healthy foundation within the home, as discussed in Chapter 5. Furthermore, parents can help introverted children develop what I call a circle of support—a visual reminder of the child's support system. This circle of support can serve as a reminder whenever the child withdraws related to his feelings of being overwhelmed. The worksheet on page 66 outlines the circle of support. Complete this with your child as a way to increase trust and build connections.

Perhaps one of the more difficult aspects of resiliency to work with is emotional sensitivity. Involving a child's emotional reactions to situations and the level of recovery a child demonstrates, emotional sensitivity can be a difficult area for introverts. As I discussed in the first section of the book, introverted children often hold in their emotions until they explode. At first glance, they may appear to be handling setbacks in stride. More often than not, they are overthinking the emotions and bottling them up inside before exploding. The stress response for the introvert often takes longer to trigger than it does in his or her extroverted peers. However, introverts are more uncomfortable with the feelings associated with a stress response, resulting in a larger, more intense reaction to relatively low levels of anxiety or stress.

Recovery time, like processing time, may be slower with introverts. Part of this is related to their brain chemistry. They will often require downtime away from family or friends in order to reestablish an appropriate baseline. Additionally, as introverted children process so much of their world internally, it may appear that they have reachieved a calm

WORKSHEET 6

Circle of Support

Directions: List all of the places where you spend time and the people you feel safe with in each location. I have started listing a few places and people for you.

Place	Person(s)
Home	*Mom, Dad, sister, brother*
School	
Church	
Sports	

Use the list to help your child make a "circle of support" he or she can rely on when needed. It is important that introverted children know whom they can turn to for support and which people will understand them.

state when, in fact, they have not. They can reignite their emotions with small triggers and take an even longer time to achieve balance.

One of the best things a parent can do to assist in stabilizing the emotional reactivity of their introverted children is to teach and support healthy habits. Getting enough sleep and exercise can help children maintain emotional control. Furthermore, paying close attention to eating habits, with an emphasis on balanced diets, can provide the biological support introverts need in regulating their emotions.

Figure 5 outlines some of the healthy habits introverts need in order to thrive. Helping your child focus on these things can assist you as you nurture his or her developing resiliency skills.

All in all, parents play a large role in developing and nurturing resiliency in children. Focusing on teaching self-efficacy skills, developing autonomy and discernment, building supportive relationships, and managing emotional reactivity are all things that can assist the introverted child in developing resiliency. This topic will come up again as we explore other aspects of introversion, including the social aspects of introversion and supporting our children as they become their own unique individuals.

Class Notes: Building a Resilient Classroom Environment

Just as it is important to nurture resiliency in the home, it is also important to create a learning environment that fosters resiliency. Much of this can be accomplished in how the educator runs the classroom. To develop autonomy and mastery, the educator can include choice within activities for some lessons. Choice can also be introduced within set parameters, including seat location or the types of rewards the student is earning. The inclusion of choice enables the introverted child to exert some level of control over his surroundings, increasing resiliency. Allowing for "safe" risk-taking in the classroom, including a focus on process (not just grades and tests), will develop stronger self-efficacy skills and strengthen overall resiliency.

This chart reflects the components of a healthy and balanced lifestyle. How many habits are you using? Are you helping your child learn healthy habits?

Habit	Why It's Important	Considerations
Proper Rest	Introverts require sleep in order to renew their energy stores. Getting 8 hours of sleep nightly (at minimum) ensures proper brain functioning and mood stabilization.	Turn off electronics and develop a bedtime routine to assist with sleep troubles.
Eat Healthy Foods	Introverts perform best when they are eating many small meals filled with protein. The protein hits throughout the day help stabilize energy.	When introverts are run down, they will naturally crave simple sugars and refined foods. These can make the energy drain happen faster and should be avoided.
Daily Exercise	Introverts tend to live in their heads, forgoing activity. But, getting exercise on a daily basis, even small amounts, will assist in recharging dwindling energy supplies and managing stress.	Any type of activity is good for introverts. But be careful about exercising late at night as this can lead to sleep problems.
Relaxation and Connections	Introverts need a balance of solitude and connections in order to achieve optimal balance. Take time to help your child both destress and renew, as well as connect on a social level.	If you find your child (or yourself) withdrawing from all social contact or becoming agitated, check their stress levels. Odds are their energy stores have been depleted related to stress. Help them take a little time to decompress and renew.

Figure 5. Healthy habits for introverts.

I previously stated that balancing small-group activities with individual activities was an essential aspect of meeting the needs of both the introvert and the extrovert. This balancing of social demands can also assist with resiliency. Providing opportunities for meaningful collaboration with like-minded peers, along with establishing a "no-bullying" classroom environment will ensure that the introverted student is able to benefit from the naturally occurring social connections as a way to enhance resiliency.

Educators can also teach children emotional control within the school setting. The current educational trend of schoolwide behavior intervention systems focuses on teaching social skills that build competencies in the areas of emotional reactivity and recovery. Teaching children what behavioral expectations are, how to react appropriately to negative emotional impulses, and how to manage their behavior are all factors that will have a positive impact on resiliency in the classroom. Introverts, in particular, benefit from directed teaching in these areas as it appeals to their natural tendency for self-talk and internal regulation.

In the next chapter, I will address how to create safe classrooms, a skill that will enhance the resiliency strategies mentioned here.

NURTURING RESILIENCY Q&A

As I've mentioned throughout this chapter, resiliency refers to the ability to bounce back from setbacks and adjust to life's curveballs. As parents, it is a skill we can help our children develop. Focusing on helping our children develop a strong sense of self, manage their emotions, and build strong relationships with others are all things that can enhance their resiliency.

The following questions are ones that have come up during recent parent trainings and speak to a lot of the pressures parents may feel when it comes to assisting their children in developing this skill.

Will the mistakes I make as a parent ruin my poor child for life?

This is one of the most common worries I hear from parents—the fear that somehow a decision you make will cause irreparable damage to your children. In truth, all parents cause some amount of damage to the emotional well-being of their children, in the same way that all spouses cause some measure of emotional pain in their partner. I know this is not what you expected me to say, but it is the truth. So, now that we have that out of the way, you can stop worrying about it.

Yes, seriously, stop worrying. We, as parents, do not have all of the answers to our children. We will get mad when we shouldn't, we may say things we'd like to take back, and we will let them down in some way. The sooner we accept that, the sooner we can move past the parent guilt and pressure the majority of us feel and move forward to the business of being the best parents we can in any given moment. By accepting that we are not going to be perfect as parents, we can let go of the pressure and shift our focus to trying to be conscious parents, mindful of our children's needs. By being mindful and discerning, we are able to "see" the situations with more clarity and help our children.

So stop the parent guilt and focus on being the best you can in the moment. Ask questions, read books, and enhance your skills. The rest will take care of itself.

What are some indicators that my introverted child is resilient?

Resiliency typically encompasses three distinct attributes, including one's belief that he or she has some autonomy over the environment, the ability to build meaningful connections, and mastery over one's emotions. It is the same with introverts. Helping your child to develop these attributes is one way to ensure the development of strong resiliency.

Answer the questions on page 71 in order to evaluate your child's resiliency strength and weaknesses. If you find some areas of weakness, reread the chapter and focus in on some of the strategies to build that area.

QUESTIONNAIRE 3

How Resilient Are My Children?

1. My child has one or two close friends who understand and support him or her.
   - ❏ *True*   ❏ *False*

2. My child has the problem-solving skills needed to work through typical social issues or conflicts.
   - ❏ *True*   ❏ *False*

3. My child knows who to turn to for support when things are hard.
   - ❏ *True*   ❏ *False*

4. My child is typically optimistic about his or her future.
   - ❏ *True*   ❏ *False*

5. My child is able to manage his or her emotions and recover from setbacks.
   - ❏ *True*   ❏ *False*

Once you are finished, take a moment to reflect on your answers. What are the areas of strength for your child? What are areas of concern? Take a moment to write down your thoughts regarding resiliency.

What is the best way for me, as the parent, to foster resiliency in my introverted child?

Resiliency develops when children feel safe in their environment. As discussed in Chapter 6, introverts feel safest within the home environment when predictable routines are in place and parental reactions are predictable. When this is established, introverted children naturally develop resiliency.

Life, however, is seldom predictable or routine. So how can you help your introverted child prepare for the inevitable curveballs that life will toss? The answer, I believe, lies in the strategies mentioned earlier in the chapter. Focusing on the healthy habits on page 68, as well as teaching and practicing the hula hoop technique (page 64) will give your children a strong foundation for resiliency. Helping your children develop a sense of autonomy over their environment, as well as learning to manage their unique temperament and understand their introversion, are all things that will further develop their resiliency and prepare them for adulthood.

As a parent, how can I help my introverted child see herself as being strong and not just "shy"?

Ah yes, the "shyness" factor. Many parents of introverts worry that their child will forever see herself as shy. As I mentioned in the first section of the book, shyness actually has little to do with temperament. It is a learned behavior and although it is certainly more common in introverts related to how they interact with the world, it is not a defining feature of introversion.

Helping your introverted child go beyond any shyness she may exhibit goes back to the strategies of building autonomy and learning about her unique attributes of temperament. The more the child can understand what it means to be introverted, the more she can develop her many strengths and push against the societal norm that she "should be" more extroverted. That isn't to say that the introverted child should not learn how to "play extrovert" when needed. As I mentioned earlier, there are times when it is important to be more outgoing and "extroverted." I will discuss this even further in Part IV of this book.

Is resiliency something that can impact learning? How?

Yes, resiliency can certainly impact a child's ability to learn. Learning is innately a risk-laden activity. Every time new information is presented, the learner must be willing to take some amount of risk that he will be able to learn the new information and demonstrate mastery of that material. A person's willingness to take these types of intellectual risks is related to resiliency.

As I've mentioned throughout the chapter, one of the main attributes of resiliency is related to feeling a sense of mastery over one's environment. Self-efficacy, problem-solving abilities, and adaptability—all things required as part of the learning process—are areas that contribute to the child's overall belief in his ability to control some aspect of life. When children fail to develop skills in these areas, school can cease to be a safe place. And when this happens, learning suffers.

So what can an educator do? Focus on helping all students, including those with introverted temperaments, learn how to take academic risks. Create an environment in which learning is not strictly measured by performance on a test or statewide assessment, but also on the process of learning. Finally, teach creative problem solving and "out-of-the-box" thinking, something most introverts do well; innovation is born from these skills.

In a Nutshell . . .

Big Ideas

- ❖ Resiliency involves the following attributes: autonomy over the environment, meaningful connections with others, and appropriate emotional regulation.
- ❖ Developing resiliency means strengthening the above attributes.
- ❖ Introverts may struggle in any or all of the areas of resiliency.
- ❖ Despite some difficulties introverted children may have initially, many attributes of introversion correlate with strong resiliency over a lifetime.

❖ Parents and parenting style has a strong influence over the development of resiliency.

Supplemental Charts, Tips, and Worksheets
❖ Tip Sheet 5: Sharing Control—page 63
❖ Tip Sheet 6: The Hula Hoop Technique—page 64
❖ Worksheet 6: Circle of Support—page 66
❖ Figure 5: Healthy Habits for Introverts—page 68
❖ Questionnaire 3: How Resilient Are My Children?—page 71

chapter 7

Building a Stronger Village

"My sister drives me crazy. She always wants to talk, talk, talk."—Caleb, Age 14

We've all heard the phrase "it takes a village." When it comes to raising children it does . . . but not just any village, a strong village. And in a diverse home and world, the more everyone can learn about tolerance and balancing the needs of everyone, the better.

Enter your family. In Chapter 1, you completed a worksheet to tell you everyone's temperament in the household. If you are like the majority of families, you discovered that there are both introverted and extroverted children at home, as well as mixed temperament parents or caregivers. This menagerie of temperaments can pose unique challenges to today's families.

Introverted parents and caregivers have the best understanding of their introverted children. However, their road is not without potential pitfalls.

Most modern parents are juggling more than a few activities at any given time. Work, both inside and outside of the home, as well as parenting demands, leave the most organized of parents exhausted. Couple this with the normal energy needs of the introvert, and these parents may find themselves agitated from their own lack of downtime. Oftentimes, introverted parents will wear out their energy reserves, resulting in a need for quiet and renewal that they may or may not be able to meet. This can be particularly problematic when the introverted parent has extroverted children whose natural chatty nature only drains the parent further.

Extroverted parents are better equipped to handle the social hustle and bustle of modern parenting. But they often do not understand the needs of their introverted children or spouses. The extroverted parent thrives on external connections, activity, and general busyness. He or she will typically overschedule every moment of a trip or outing, not realizing the toll this may be taking on the introverted members of the household. An example of this that immediately comes to mind is my father. When he and my mother lived in Hawaii, they came to the mainland every 3 or 4 months to visit. However, my father usually filled their schedule so full that I would be lucky to get even one day with my mom. He wasn't doing this to be insensitive to either of our needs, he just liked being that busy. It took Mom and me months to help him understand that we could not function that way. We needed time, just Mom and I, to enjoy each other's company. Quietly.

In addition to the problem of overscheduling that can occur, extroverted parents are often confused by the actions of their introverted spouses and children. They may perceive their spouse's need to retreat to the bedroom after a busy day as an act of abandonment, rather than a need to renew. They may see their introverted children as lonely and isolated because they seldom go out with friends. And they may see the constant contemplation an introvert often exchanges in as folly. In truth, the two merely look at the world from very unique lenses.

Mixed temperament siblings also pose challenges in the home. Introverted siblings, although tolerant of their introverted brothers and sisters, may retreat too often, requiring excessive isolation. The collective energy of introverted siblings may be too low by the end of a week. This can be made even worse if the parents are also introverted and experiencing energy lows. In these moments, the introverts would benefit from the higher energy levels of the extrovert.

Introverted siblings may get overly snippy with each other as they both become overwhelmed from a particularly chaotic week. Take, for example, the family of all introverts on a Friday night. Odds are really good every member of the household is tucked away in his or her own personal space basically ignoring one another. Or they are quick to get angry with each other related to pent-up frustrations caused by their personal energy drains.

Extroverted siblings share similar issues to the extroverted parent. They often misunderstand their introverted kin, interpreting the introvert's need for downtime as abandonment. Furthermore, they may feel at odds with the introvert, miscuing every action from their extroverted point of view.

So how can parents assist in regulating and strengthening the family unit in the midst of mixed temperaments? One way is by understanding the various needs of the family members. In my household, for example, I have one extroverted daughter in a family of introverts. It can be very hard on her as the rest of the household often craves peace and quiet at the same time that she is craving connections. To better meet her need to connect, I started a "transition" routine for myself when I leave work, going to my local coffee house for 20 minutes of unwinding time before I come home. In that way, I am emotionally ready to have her tell me about her day and connect with me in the way that I know she needs as soon as I get home.

Sometimes the stress of modern society overwhelms even the strongest of families. Economic hardships, illness, divorce, and other stressors can leave parents and children frustrated and unsettled. This can be particularly problematic with introverts, as they need the sanctuary of a calm home environment in order to renew each day. Parents can help introverted children find a measure of peace even within the extreme stressors some families are forced to face. The key lies in helping introverted children understand how stress affects them in general, as well as what they can do about it.

Stress is most typically defined as the physical, mental, or emotional response to environmental demands that result in some form of physical tension. A stress response can happen as a result of negative events (like a fight with a parent or friend or loss of the family home), positive events (performing in a dance recital or high school graduation), or more neutral events (playing a high-action video game or seeing an action-packed movie). Regardless of the trigger—negative, positive, or neutral—a person's stress response is basically the same. And temperament can influence that response.

As I have mentioned previously in the book, extroverts are hardwired to utilize dopamine and their fight-or-flight response system more than their introverted counterparts. Because of this, they tend to live in a heightened stress state, often falling into their personal stress response easily and readily. They enjoy the feelings caused by the adrenal rush—the rapid heart rate, sweaty palms, tight muscles. They enjoy feeling "ready for action" at all times and will often seek out activities that can give them that rush. Until they burn out, that is. Then they tend to hide and withdraw, unable to process their stress response in the same way.

Introverts take much longer to activate their stress cycle. Because they are deep thinkers and have a natural tendency to think through things, they often prevent large-scale stress reactions completely, rationalizing their concerns away. That sounds positive, right? And it is. Most of the time. Sometimes, however, their stress cycles creep up on them and leave them unable to cope, all with minimal clues that it is about to happen.

Why does this occur?

Introverts are uncomfortable with even small amounts of stress. The pressures felt during a test may be enough for them to shut down and withdraw or become overly agitated. Large issues like divorce and economic hardship almost always trigger a significant stress response in introverts. And unlike their extroverted peers, introverts will do almost anything to avoid and get rid of the stressful feelings. Unfortunately, the quickest way to rid the body of the physical effects of stress is through physical exertion—something most introverts also avoid when overwhelmed.

Parents can do a lot to assist introverted children in dealing with stress, whether the source of the stress is from home or elsewhere. First, listen to what your children are saying about their stress. Because introverted children are constantly thinking, they often can isolate the source of their stress. That is not to say that they are always correct in their interpretation of what they are feeling. There are times when they will not be. Regardless of their accuracy, knowing their point of view with regard to their stress will give you a place to start when coaching them on better ways to manage the feelings.

Next, it is important that parents revisit the hula hoop technique (page 64) from Chapter 6. This strategy will help introverted children learn to discern things they can control from the things they can't. It will give them the gift of perspective. Focusing on the things you can control and learning to release the things you have no control over is one of the best ways to manage stress.

Once that strategy is revisited and retaught, if needed, the focus should be on teaching relaxation techniques. One of the difficult aspects of a person's stress cycle is what happens to cognition. As the stress increases and the emotions begin to spiral, the child's ability to rationally process information declines. Blood flow shifts away from the frontal lobe in the brain, reducing logical thinking and problem-solving skills. What is needed at this point is the gift of time in order to improve cognition. This can happen by relaxing.

There are several methods of relaxation that work well with introverted children, including the four listed on the tip sheet on page 80. Each serves its own purpose and each should be taught to the child. These particular forms of relaxation work well with introverted children as they rely on the innate thinking and self-talk that is common with introverts.

In addition to learning *how* to relax, introverted children need to learn how to tell if they *are* relaxed. I cannot tell you how often I ask introverted children to tell me if they are relaxed or not, only to discover their own assessment of their internal state is a little skewed when they are in the midst of a stress cycle. The worksheet on page 81 can help children learn which questions to ask themselves as they learn to take control over their stress cycles and responses.

One thing that you may want to do is have both the relaxation tip sheet and the worksheet laminated on a small card that your children can carry in their wallets, backpacks, or purses. They may enjoy the little reminder without having to speak with you or anyone else about it.

Sometimes the stress is too much to handle, resulting in significant behavioral outbursts. When this happens, parents and children are at

TIP SHEET 7

Relaxation 101

The following strategies are great ways to relax. They require nothing other than your thoughts and a few calm moments:

- ❖ **Deep Breathing**: Take several slow, deep breaths. Imagine the stress physical symptoms "melting away."
- ❖ **Breathing Colors**: Take several deep breaths. On the inhalation, picture your favorite color. I use blue or pink. On the exhalation, imagine a dirty color. This is the color of the stress in your body. Continue slow steady breathing until the color you inhale matches the color you exhale.
- ❖ **Mini-Vacations**: Picture your favorite place in the world. Imagine everything about that place—how things look, how they feel, how they smell. The more vivid, the better.
- ❖ **Mental Rehearsal**: This is particularly helpful before a test or performance-based activity. Imagine taking each step of the activity successfully. For example, if you are preparing for a piano recital, you may picture getting ready for the recital, walking on stage, sitting on the piano bench, hearing the music in your mind, and playing the music.

odds as the situation spirals into a yelling match or worse. Although outgoing extroverts are usually thought of as being the ones most likely to engage in acting-out behaviors, introverts are not above some of these behaviors as well. This is especially true when they are overwhelmed and have not taken time to renew their energy supplies and decompress. At these times, the introverted child will be rigid and belligerent in the home setting. Behavior you may never see in public or at school will suddenly happen in the "safety" of the home setting, including yelling, disrespectful backtalk, and worse. This can be highly challenging for parents to handle, especially if you are also overextended with little time for renewal.

WORKSHEET 7

Am I Relaxed?

Directions: Read each statement and decide if you agree or disagree.

	I agree	I disagree	I neither agree nor disagree
1. I am relaxed in my body, with no tense areas.			
2. My mind is relaxed and focused.			
3. I am not feeling any strong emotions. I am calm.			
4. I feel confident and ready to move forward.			

Based on your answers, are you fully relaxed? Did you use one of the relaxation techniques? Which one? Was it effective? Do you need to try another one?

TIP SHEET 8

Time Away

* ❖ Take several deep breaths.
* ❖ Quiet the chatter in your thoughts.
* ❖ Focus on one thing like breathing, blocking out everything else.
* ❖ You need a moment of time to regain control of your feelings; give yourself permission to take that time.

Behavioral outbursts are best handled before the outburst occurs, by teaching your introverted child how to renew and relax. But when that isn't enough and the outburst is already occurring, there are a few things you can do to help calm things down and restore order. First, give yourself permission to disengage from the problem, even when the problem is extreme disrespect aimed right at you. By disengaging from the problem, you are able to keep your own stress cycle from flaring and to objectively think through the crisis.

Sometimes your child has already hooked you into the outburst. This is very common when the behavioral problem begins with challenges to your respect or authority. At this point, it is very helpful to give yourself—and your child—time away, particularly when you are working with the introverted child. You all need a chance to breathe, calm down, and get your blood flowing back into your frontal lobe. The tip sheet above gives additional tips for effective ways to take a break during a crisis.

Once you are calm and thinking clearly, assess the situation to ensure that there are no safety issues. Then, leave the upset introvert alone. No matter what he is saying to you, let it go, disengage, and allow the situation to deescalate before you engage further. Like I said before, this will be difficult for many parents. But, there is nothing to be gained by engaging when the child is explosive. Give the situation time—sometimes minutes, sometimes hours, or longer—to calm. Above everything else, stay emotionally detached during these difficult periods. It is the best thing to do, for you and your child.

Stage of Behavioral Crisis	Actions to Take	Goal
Before the Crisis	• Teach your child how to manage his or her emotions • Learn the warning signs of your child's escalation cycle • Teach your child how to relax	Prevent escalation from occurring
During the Crisis	• Detach emotionally from the crisis • Remain calm • Keep safety in mind • Ignore minor problems	Manage the problem behavior safely and deescalate the crisis as soon as possible
After the Crisis	• Debrief after everyone is calm and the crisis is over • Review strategies for managing emotions with your child	View the crisis as a teachable moment and determine an action plan to prevent future problems

Figure 6. Dealing with difficult behaviors.

Figure 6 provides a quick visual reminder of how to handle behavioral outbursts when they occur. Use the techniques in the chart anytime the behaviors occur, focusing on finding ways to prevent them from occurring in the first place.

Class Notes: Using PBIS Strategies With Introverts

Behavior difficulties are not limited to home settings. As you well know, difficult behaviors can show up at school, too. Most of the time, however, these behaviors are not happening with your introverts, but with the extroverted children. Perhaps that is the reason that the trend in positive behavioral interventions and supports, or PBIS, focuses a lot on strategies that are effective with extroverts. External reward systems, role-playing of new skills, and open communication between teachers and students when there is a behavior problem are all highly effective strategies to use with extroverts.

But what about the introverted children in the classroom? Is any part of the traditional PBIS model effective with them?

Absolutely! PBIS is all about teaching children what the social and behavioral expectations are in various situations, along with explicitly teaching the skills. This is definitely something that would appeal to the introvert. Knowing the expectations and having a clear understanding of behavioral expectations in various locations, as well as clear guidelines regarding consequences are all things that increase the comfort of the introvert. In this way, the PBIS model can be very helpful in establishing a classroom setting that can support both the extrovert and the introvert.

So how can you establish this model in your classroom? I could write a book on the topic of PBIS. In fact, several people have.

In short, PBIS for the classroom starts by focusing on determining expectations for behavior by location, and then systematically teaching and reteaching the skills needed to meet the expectation. Rewards are given to those who are able to comply with the expectations. Behavior data is used to determine those students who may require additional supports in developing behavioral skills and meeting the classroom expectations. More specific information regarding PBIS can be found in the Resources section at the end of the book.

DEALING WITH FAMILY STRESSORS Q&A

We live in a busy and stressful world. With the current economic pressures, as well as dynamic changes in family structures, many children are living with levels of stress previously reserved for adults. Pressures to perform, changes in societal norms regarding behavior, and lack of social skills teaching has created a potential maelstrom for children.

The following questions focus on the stress typically experienced by children in our modern culture.

How do introverted children manifest stress, particularly when they are young?

Introverted children, as I've mentioned before, tend to keep their emotions locked inside. Many times parents won't realize how stressed they are until they finally blow up. That said, here are some signs that a meltdown may be coming soon:

- sudden sleep problems;
- increased withdrawal;
- edginess;
- eating more sugary or carb-loaded foods;
- increased sensitivity to sounds, sights, and/or smells; and
- inability to self-sooth or accept help from others.

All of these things may indicate that the introverted child is experiencing higher than normal stress. When stress levels reach their boiling point, an explosion is the typical outcome, as the child's ability to cope with environmental demands is eclipsed.

How do I help my introverted child deal with the common stressors in a busy, modern family?

As I mentioned earlier, families are busier than ever these days. Parents are working multiple jobs to make ends meet. Children are involved in school, sports, faith groups, and other activities as parents succumb to pressure to make sure there is no downtime for children to waste playing video games or getting involved with the "wrong crowd." Time together as a family is at a premium.

How does the introverted child fair in this too-busy lifestyle that now defines most households? The short answer, they don't. Not well, at least. Introverted children need downtime. When it is not provided, they grow increasingly frustrated and withdrawn. Their emotions begin to run amuck and eventually they explode.

Additionally, introverted children thrive when they have deep connections to those around them. I will never forget some of the words my introverted teenager has said to me, asking me to spend more quality time with her. She was right, of course; I had gotten sucked into my own introversion and buried myself in my writing. What we both needed was a little time connecting together.

For additional strategies to help introverted children deal with stress, take a look at the tips listed on page 87. Practice any of the strategies the next time things are overwhelming your introvert.

What are the warning signs that something may be "wrong" with my introverted child?

Whenever I meet with parents, I am always asked for warning signs that something may be "wrong." I think this is the incorrect approach. We always see what we expect to see, so if we are expecting to see something "wrong," then we shouldn't be surprised when we see it. Instead, I prefer to focus on knowing who our children are at their core—their authentic selves. Focusing on this allows us to see the child first, not the behavior or "problems."

That said, it is important to be aware of indicators that the child may be headed for a serious problem. Similar to the symptoms of stress previously discussed, although at an increased level of intensity, stressed introverts often appear agitated, quick to temper, stubborn, and frustrated. They will typically be resistant to accepting help, rigid in their thinking, and act like a time bomb waiting to go off!

Intervening at this point can be difficult, as the introverted child is often unwilling to accept anything that will mediate the stress. Recognizing the subtle changes in the child's behavior before it gets to this point is the best way to assist the child and prevent a serious blow up later.

My introverted child seems anxious all of the time. Is she more likely to develop an anxiety problem and what can I do to help her?

As strange as it may seem, extroverts are hardwired to experience higher levels of anxiety as compared to introverts. This is related to their

TIP SHEET 9
Introverts and Stress

- ❖ Focus on healthy habits including appropriate eating, sleeping, and exercise routines.
- ❖ Spend time relaxing every day. Don't allow your energy stores to become too depleted.
- ❖ Pay attention to your internal chatter. Redirect negative self-talk.
- ❖ Be mindful and realistic in your perspective of situations and guard against perfectionism.
- ❖ If you find yourself particularly stressed over a specific event, mentally rehearse the event, focusing on successfully completing the activity.

dependence on the fight or flight response. But extroverts are also better equipped to live in that state of anxiety. It feels good to them.

Introverts, on the other hand, rely on the part of the nervous system responsible for rest. Because of this, small amounts of anxiety can feel overwhelming. So while the introvert is less likely to develop anxiety problems, she is more likely to be overwhelmed by "normal" anxious moments. You can help her with this by teaching her the relaxation techniques outlined earlier in the chapter. Teaching her to both recognize her stress and know how to minimize the impact is the key to helping her learn lifelong strategies for managing the stress from whatever life throws her way.

School can also be a stressful environment for some of my students. Is there something I should do to help my introverted students cope with the stress?

Performance-related stress can be a huge obstacle for any child. And introverts often react more strongly to stressors than their extroverted counterparts. Educators can help the introverted child by implementing some of the strategies previously discussed, like setting up a calming environment and normalizing academic risks. Balancing out the types of activities between group and independent and timed and untimed tasks can also go a long way to help the introvert. Finally, teaching all children how to manage test anxiety using relaxation techniques and test-taking strategies can be of great assistance to the introverted student. Part III goes into each of these in greater depth.

In a Nutshell . . .

Big Ideas

- ❖ Parents respond differently to introverted children based on their own temperaments.
- ❖ Siblings respond differently to each other based on temperament.
- ❖ Environmental stress can impact family functioning.
- ❖ Introverts deal with stress through withdrawal, frustration, and eventually, behavioral outbursts.
- ❖ Parents can teach introverted children how to deal with stress.
- ❖ When behavioral outbursts do occur, disengagement can be an effective strategy until tempers cool.
- ❖ PBIS strategies address the needs of both extroverts and introverts.

Supplemental Pages

- ❖ Tip Sheet 7: Relaxation 101—page 80
- ❖ Worksheet 7: Am I Relaxed?—page 81
- ❖ Tip Sheet 8: Time Away—page 82
- ❖ Figure 6: Dealing With Difficult Behaviors—page 83
- ❖ Tip Sheet 9: Introverts and Stress—page 87

chapter 8

In Their Own Words

Introverts and Extroverts, Oh My!

Most households include both introverts and extroverts, including my own. Needless to say, differences in temperament can intensify sibling rivalries. This next story is taken from a conversation that occurred during a parenting workshop several years ago. In that training, parents and their children worked together to decipher the ways in which extroversion and introversion impacted their family. As with the other stories, the names and identifying information have been changed to respect the privacy of the training participants.

Here are some details about the family itself. The mother, Katherine, works from home, and the father, Daniel, works out of town, commuting more than 2 hours daily. There are two children in the family, both girls, ages 8 and 12. Katherine has identified herself and her 8-year-old daughter as being introverts and has identified Daniel and their 12-year-old as extroverts.

The following represents the family's answers to several questions asked during a parenting workshop. Their answers provide insight into how one family deals with the needs of multiple temperaments in the home.

What is a typical evening like at home?

Katherine: Most nights we have soccer, dance, or other extracurricular activities. We spend time driving around from activity to activity. We are home around 7 p.m. on any given night. The girls settle into homework by 8 p.m. and we try to get them to bed by 10.

Daniel: Katherine disappears before then. She is just tired every night. She goes into the room and watches television with the door closed.

Katherine: I'm not tired. I just need some quiet time. But I don't always get it. By that time of night, the girls are getting on each other's nerves. They argue a lot, and Daniel and I get tired of playing referee. They share a room together, so sending them to their room isn't always an option. I get really tired of the arguments night after night, but we, Daniel and I, don't know how to solve the problem.

Are there any problems that come up that you think are related to temperament?

Daniel: Based on what I've learned here about introversion and extroversion, I think the arguing has a lot to do with it. Also, Katherine and I aren't always on the same page when it comes to how to deal with the kids. She thinks its fine that our youngest daughter never socializes on the weekends. I think she needs more friends. I want her to be like our oldest, with lots of social activities.

Katherine: Just because she isn't on the phone all night doesn't mean she doesn't have friends, Daniel. See, this is another example of the temperament thing—Daniel and I have really different opinions of why certain things happen in the house. I will tell you this, I am certain now the fighting that happens between the kids is related to introversion.

Tell me a little bit more about that. How intense does it get?

Katherine: It can get really bad: both girls yelling, both girls crying. It's a mess. But I think a lot of it has to do with sharing a room. Based on what we're learning about introverts needing time alone and extroverts needing to connect, I think that is a root cause for a lot of the arguments and tension between the girls—they are each trying to reenergize, but they need something different to make that happen.

Daniel: I think it would be worth it to separate the girls and give them their own rooms. At this point, it is just not working with them sharing a room. Katherine?

Katherine: I agree. Maybe we can try that, along with insisting on a little downtime for me.

Two weeks and two classes later, I asked Katherine and Daniel if there had been any positive changes since the girls got their own rooms and since the family tried implementing a few of the strategies discussed in the workshop.

Now that you have implemented a set time for renewal and given the girls their own rooms, have there been any positive changes?

Katherine: Definitely! The girls are getting along much better now that they don't share a room. I even notice that the youngest is willing to spend time with her sister more often. Of course, they still argue. Especially right after we all get home. But it is beginning to get better.

Daniel: I think splitting the girls was the right choice. I still worry about the oldest. I feel like she doesn't get enough of Katherine's time. But I think everyone is really making an effort to understand each other's temperament and respect each other's boundaries.

Katherine: Yes, we are all really trying.

What advice would you give other families with regard to temperament?

Katherine: First, figure out who are the extroverts and introverts in the family. It makes such a difference to really understand everyone's temperament. Then, look for ways to make both feel comfortable: for the extrovert, look for ways to help them connect; for the introvert, look for ways to allow them to be alone. It'll help the whole family unit if everyone can get opportunities to renew that work with their unique personality.

Daniel: Yeah, and don't assume that just because you like to be alone at the end of the day, that everyone does. For the parents, if you and your spouse have different temperaments, don't take your different needs as personal. It probably isn't personal at all. Also, be willing to learn something new. When Katherine and I started the workshop, I was pretty certain there was little I was going to learn. I mean, we were good parents, so taking the class sort of felt like a waste. But, I was wrong. I learned so much about myself and each other. And our family has really benefitted from everything, especially the whole idea of understanding the various temperaments and thinking about them when parenting.

Extroverts and introverts can struggle in their relationships with each other. This can be especially true in a family setting. This chapter pointed to one family's experiences with temperament and some of the strategies that have been utilized. The preceding chapters highlighted even more strategies that can help provide a good foundation in which every member of the household can thrive.

part III

Introverted Kids at School

As I mentioned previously, Western culture celebrates extroverted behavior. Schools are microcosms designed to promote extroverted behaviors. High-stakes testing is geared toward the ways extroverts tend to learn. Competition and collaboration, both well-suited for the extrovert, has replaced innovation and creativity as the norm of our educational system. It's no wonder that schools can provide a unique challenge to our introverted children. This can be particularly true for both gifted children and those with learning challenges.

The upcoming chapters examine introverted children at school, addressing how introverts learn, the common misperceptions that happen in the educational environment, dealing with competition, and dealing with failure.

As we begin to evaluate the introvert in the school setting, I want you to take a moment and reflect on your thoughts about your introverted child and school. Take a moment to answer the questionnaire on page 94 before moving into this section.

QUESTIONNAIRE 4

Ideas About Learning and the Introvert

1. My introverted child feels that school is . . . (*complete the sentence*).

2. I think my child's schooling has been . . . (*complete the sentence*).

3. I believe teachers understand temperament and think about that as they work with my child.
    ❏ *True*   ❏ *False*

4. I believe that my child could do better at school than he or she does.
    ❏ *True*   ❏ *False*

5. I think schools are geared more toward extroverts.
    ❏ *True*   ❏ *False*

6. If I answered "true" above, I think the biggest difficulties facing introverts at school are . . . (*complete the sentence*).

    Once you are finished, take a moment to reflect on your answers and consider the following questions: What, if anything, would you like to see change for your child at school? What type of schooling does your child currently participate in—homeschooling, charter schools, private schools, traditional public school? Do you think one or the other is of more benefit to your introverted child? Take a moment to write down your thoughts regarding temperament and your goals for this book.

chapter 9

How Introverts Learn

"I hate it when teachers put me on the spot in class by asking me questions in front of everyone. I never know what to say."—Chandler, Age 15

The classroom—it plays such a large role in our children's lives. A place where they learn far more than just reading, writing, and arithmetic, modern-day school campuses are also one of the primary socialization environments for children. As extroverts make up as much as 75% of the general population according to some researchers (Laney, 2002), it's reasonable to assume that there are three extroverted students for each introverted student in the typical school. What does this mean for the introvert? Like elsewhere in society, the introverted child is likely the minority and is typically misunderstood.

Introverts, as I have mentioned previously, often present with two distinct personas—the mask they wear for the world, and the authentic person beneath the mask. Their outer mask helps them function in a world that seldom appreciates the quiet strengths of introversion.

But not without a price.

The mask works as a barrier to the near-constant bombardment of sensory stimuli most introverts are faced with in all aspects of their public lives, especially the classroom. Often noisy and highly visually stimulating, the classroom can overwhelm introverted students long before instruction has even begun. The mask most introverts wear enables them to detach from both the physical stimulation caused by the senses and the emotional stimulation that comes from spending large amounts of time with extroverts.

Unfortunately, the mask also gives the wrong impression to others, including teachers. Many may characterize the introverted learner as overly aloof or disinterested in learning. Sometimes the introvert is thought of as unmotivated or a loner. In truth, the introverted student is just trying to find a way to fit into the extroverted school setting and survive. He typically enjoys learning and is capable of making deep connections with the material and can offer deeper levels of conversation and debate than many of his extroverted counterparts. That is, when the classroom supports mixed temperaments.

Introverts are deep thinkers, as I've previously stated. Because of this, they tend to engage in much inner dialogue about the material being taught. They are often the students who will remain quiet at the start of educational discussions, only to offer profound insight toward the end of the conversations. In this way, they can often "fool" the teacher into thinking they are unmotivated or not understanding the material. In truth, they often just need ample processing time in order to participate fully in conversations.

This type of learning, having deep inner dialogues regarding the material and offering insight during instructional discourse, is great in high school honors classes or in college. But what about the elementary- and middle school-level classrooms? In these settings, lessons are often taught in bite-sized chunks with an emphasis on rote learning, automaticity, and assessments. Timed tests are used to develop mastery in areas like math and spelling. Short-term memory is stretched with immediate feedback assessments. These are not areas of strength for many introverts.

If the classroom strategies are not balanced between using these types of assessments along with short-answer assessments, projects, and more in-depth measures of mastery, the introvert may appear as though she is not learning the material.

What's the solution? Balanced classrooms that allow for measures of mastery that enhance multiple temperaments and multiple learning modalities. In short, classrooms with variety within assignments and assessments.

Don't get me wrong—I think it is important for every learner to become adept at taking a timed test that pulls on information in her short-term memory. But I also believe that the application of knowledge to new situations, something introverts are hard-wired to do more efficiently, is of equal importance. When the introvert has the opportunity to make deep connections within the material, he or she is able to more fully connect to the learning environment overall. This, in turn, makes him or her much more comfortable and "safe" in the school setting. And as we discussed in Part II, feeling safe and comfortable is exactly what the introvert needs to flourish within any environment.

Another aspect of introversion and learning relates to the current practice of collaborative learning groups. Throughout current Western culture, both in the workplace and in the school setting, collaboration is being used as the example of how people should work. "Two heads are better than one" seems to be the battle cry currently used in our schools. Teachers form pair-share groups to edit each others' papers. Group projects and oral presentations have become the norm, all as a way to prepare students for the working world where collaboration is king.

Although I completely agree that all students should learn how to work in a collaborative setting, it is important to understand that extroverted and introverted students approach group work in very different ways. Extroverts tend to have lively discussions over material, presenting counterarguments and alternate points of view. Introverts, on the other hand, are more collaborative in their approach to group work, seeking solutions to differences of opinions and reconciling multiple points of view (Nussbaum, 2004). Depending on the teacher's point of view regarding her purpose for the group experience, introverts may appear to not be meeting group expectations.

Furthermore, working in collaborative groups does not always promote independence. Nor is it necessarily the only path to innovation or deeper learning. Many introverts struggle with group work, especially if the group is larger than one or two additional students, or if there are particularly strong extroverts within the group. The introverted student may shut down, withdraw, or become frustrated, all resulting in inhibited learning.

The key, like with other aspects of learning, is balance. Introverted students should participate in structured group activities, as well as be given time to independently explore topics of interest and work individually on assignments. All students would balance from this approach, especially introverts.

So what can you, as the parent, do to assist the teacher and the school in establishing a balanced approach to learning in the classroom? The first thing, I believe, is to make sure you fully understand how your child learns. Know the types of activities that your child excels in, as well as the things that may be initially problematic for him or her. Support your child's education by providing a consistent time and place for homework. Remember that introverts love structure; having clear structures and expectations with regard to homework time can help your introvert. Encourage your child to pursue academic interests on his or her own to enrich the learning that happens at school.

If you find that your child is struggling, reach out to the teacher and help the school understand the influence of temperament on your child's learning. Set up a time when you can speak to the teacher regarding your child's performance and develop a plan for addressing the concerns together, keeping both the child's unique learning style and temperament in mind. Make a list bulleting the way your child expresses his or her introversion. Then use the tip sheet on page 99 and meet with the teacher. Together, you can help your child be successful in school.

One of the biggest potential problem areas for introverts and learning involves risk-taking and perfectionism. As mentioned earlier, introverts are not known for their risk-taking skills. That is much more the extroverts' game. Introverts struggle with failure, especially if the failure happens around others. Because they are easily shamed, failure is often interpreted as a character flaw, something that threatens their humanity.

TIP SHEET 10

Talking With the Teacher About My Child's Introversion

- ❖ Start with mutual high regard for the teacher and educational staff, assuming that everyone is working for the good of your child.
- ❖ Discuss your concerns in clear and specific terms. Try to remain nonemotional.
- ❖ Ask what concerns the teacher has, if any.
- ❖ Develop mutual goals and a plan for working with your child that can be consistently implemented across settings.
- ❖ Discuss a time to review your child's progress.
- ❖ If there is disagreement, work through the concerns with an open mind, focused on meeting the needs of your child.

This becomes a barrier to learning, as the introverted student resists even small academic risks.

Helping the introverted child overcome the fear of failure begins with establishing a nurturing environment at home and at school. Once this has been achieved, risk-taking can be taught in incremental steps, starting with small risks that have a high probability for success. For example, if the child is afraid of taking a risk when learning his or her multiplication facts, start with the ones he or she can master quickly. As successes are achieved, the willingness to take additional risks will increase.

Another way to help introverted children take educational risks is by helping the child see the journey toward learning as the goal, not the grade. We live a culture that places an overemphasis on mastery and end results. Although these are important, they do not replace learning. Creating balance between being goal-directed, or having an emphasis on grades, and being learning-directed, or focusing on process, is vital and necessary in order to teach appropriate academic risk-taking and combat the paralyzing aspects of perfectionism.

TIP SHEET 11

Encouraging Academic Risk-Taking

- ❖ Teach and practice practical problem-solving skills.
- ❖ Praise and reinforce effort, not only results.
- ❖ Lead by example by being willing to try new things.
- ❖ Focus on the process more than the outcome.
- ❖ Ask your child the following with regard to academic risks:
  - o Is it safe to try the task and/or take the risk?
  - o What are you afraid of?
  - o What is the worst thing that could happen?

The tips above will help you support your child in taking academic risks.

Perfectionism is the extreme version of having an aversion to risk-taking. Often present in gifted introverts, striving for perfection and becoming rigid in those efforts can lead to a form of paralysis when it comes to education. My experiences with my gifted and introverted daughter, as well as my own struggles with perfectionism, have given me firsthand knowledge of the paralyzing impact of this type of perfectionism. Many a sleepless night trying to complete work has happened because I was stuck in my need to do things "perfectly."

Overcoming perfectionism relies on many of the same strategies as encouraging risk-taking, including shifting the focus from result to process. This shift often releases a perfectionist from his rigidity, allowing him to again move forward. The tip sheet on page 101 will provide additional help in overcoming the cycle of perfectionism.

Remembering how introverted children learn, as well as how they may appear in class, is important in supporting their educational progress. Furthermore, dealing with their potential aversion to risk-taking and possible perfectionism before these things become a barrier to learning can go a long way to negate the potential problems introverts may face in the educational setting.

TIP SHEET 12

Moving Past Perfectionism

❖ Teach your child about his or her introversion and perfectionism.

❖ Help your child develop realistic goals.

❖ Focus on the process, not the outcome, and teach your child to do the same.

❖ Teach your child to have a realistic view of his or her performance. Poor perception can lead to increased concerns.

❖ Teach your child to ask him- or herself the following:

   o   Is my plan realistic?

   o   What would happen if I fail?

   o   What can I do instead?

The next chapters will look at other aspects of learning, including competition and a deeper view into the introvert's perception of failure.

Class Notes: A Letter to the Teacher

Dear Teacher of My Introverted Child:

I am writing you as a concerned parent, scared about my child's future. I see my child as a deep thinker who loves to learn. I see how he likes to analyze the world and develop creative solutions to unusual problems. I see his potential.

And I am so afraid that you don't.

I am afraid that you see how different he is, how sensitive and unsure. And I fear that you see those qualities as weaknesses.

I know he can't do timed tests as well as the other children. I know a typical multiple-choice exam will never show you how much he actually knows on a given subject. And I know that his brooding nature will make you think he isn't learning.

But there is more to him than these things, things that I am afraid you don't see.

Do you see how he waits before answering you, wanting to fully digest your questions and ponder the possible answers? Do you see how he watches the other children, extracting meaning from every movement, every breath? Do you see how deeply he explores the things that interest him, how purposefully he experiences life?

Do you?

My hope is that you will understand my introverted child; that he will find in your classroom the safety he needs to blossom into more than he thinks possible. I hope that you will nurture his tender soul and give him the strength to let his introversion develop into a source of strength. I hope that you will see him as I do.

Let's work together for my child, and help him develop the skills he needs to venture into this world confident and secure.

Signed,

A concerned parent

HOW INTROVERTS LEARN Q&A

I have spent the better part of my career working in education, helping parents, teachers, and children gain meaning from their experiences as a school psychologist. It is a job that has allowed me to talk with hundreds of people about how we learn and how to teach. The questions below are a sampling of those I have been asked whenever the topic of introversion arises, both during workshops and in random e-mails that cross my desk.

What is the "ideal" educational environment for an introvert?

Similar to a question in Chapter 5, there is no recipe for creating the perfect environment in which the introvert can learn. There are just too many other variables. That being said, there are a few things within a typical classroom environment that are beneficial to introverted learners.

Classrooms tend to be overstimulating on the best of days. Desks positioned with little room between the students, as well as walls that are overdecorated with brightly colored posters and work samples, can cause a sensory overload in some introverted students. Paring down the visual stimulation slightly, at least on one wall, can provide respite for the introverted learner. Similarly, taking care to seat introverts out of high-traffic areas in the classroom can also help calm the environment.

The tips on page 104 provide additional considerations when designing an educational environment that works for introverted learners.

How can introverts survive in a classroom built for extroverts?

Although it is true that classrooms are built for extroverts, with lots of activity and stimulation, group projects, and large social gatherings, that is not the only aspect to school. Most educational settings have places for students to go at lunch and break, like the library or a classroom, affording them with a respite from the social demands. Similarly, more and more campuses are understanding the need for a balanced approach to education, both in terms of the use of group activities and in terms of allowing some choice within content areas. Teachers are beginning to differentiate for different learning patterns. This can easily be extended into differentiation for temperament.

In addition to the strategies schools are beginning to incorporate into the traditional learning environment, parents can support their introverted children by teaching them how to advocate for their needs in the classroom. Additionally, helping your child develop social competency skills, something discussed in Part IV, will help your child feel more comfortable around extroverts.

What are the main differences between how introverts and extroverts learn?

I discussed a lot of the brain chemistry differences between introverts and extroverts in earlier chapters. These differences in the uses of neurotransmitters, as well as the differences in the neuropathways themselves, affect learning. Introverts, preferring the longer pathways in the brain, take longer to process information. They prefer to think deeply and analyze prior to commenting or engaging outwardly on the information. Extroverts, by contrast, think more quickly and act almost impulsively on information. They enjoy the discourse, but don't always engage

---

TIP SHEET 13

Creating the Ideal Learning Environment

Creating a learning environment that meets the needs of all learners is a Herculean task. However, the following considerations can make your classroom more introvert-friendly while not excluding extroverted learners:

- ❖ Limit visual clutter on the walls and in the room.
- ❖ Try and create some room between desks.
- ❖ Include a time away area where introverts can get away from the bustle of the classroom.
- ❖ Seat introverts away from high traffic areas.
- ❖ Balance expectations between collaboration and individual tasks.

---

with the material in deep ways. In other words, they are into breadth of information, while introverts are into depth!

As a parent, what is the best way for me to advocate for my introverted child's educational needs?

It's important for parents to partner with schools in the education of their children. Don't assume that teachers understand temperament and learning styles simply because they are educated in the field of teaching. Unfortunately, most teacher programs only touch on learning modalities, not delving into temperament at all. The neuroscience is recent and still has not found its way into most teacher preparation programs. Furthermore, many teachers don't see the strengths of introversion, focusing instead on making introverted students more outgoing. They do not understand that introverted children have their own unique strengths (Henjum, 1982).

It is important that you share the things you learn about your child with the school. Work together to solve any problems your child is having. Refer back to the tip sheet, Talking With the Teacher About My Child's Introversion (see p. 99), to assist you in developing strong communication with the school. All of these things will help you support and advocate for your child's needs.

I am a teacher. How can I ensure that I am creating an ideal learning environment for both my introverted and extroverted learners?

Balancing the educational needs of diverse populations is challenging in the best of situations. Many times you have students with unique learning needs, temperaments, mental health considerations, economic issues, and various cultural backgrounds. To meet the needs of all children is best accomplished by balancing the types of assignments you give, the ways in which you measure mastery, and the interventions you need for students. Is this challenging? Yes! But adapting differentiation strategies and positive behavioral interventions can help you establish a classroom in which the majority of students have an equal opportunity to feel safe and learn.

In a Nutshell . . .

Big Ideas

❖ Introverts often have two personas—the public mask they wear at school and the private self they save for home.

❖ An introvert's public mask creates a barrier to the overstimulation present in a typical classroom.

❖ The introvert's public mask may give the impression of being aloof and not caring about school.

❖ Introverts actually love to learn. But they prefer depth with a few subjects over breadth of many.

❖ Introverts may struggle with group work, timed tests, and quick-answer assessments.

❖ Introverts may struggle with academic risk-taking and perfectionism.

Supplemental Pages

- ❖ Tip Sheet 10: Talking With the Teacher About My Child's Introversion—page 99
- ❖ Tip Sheet 11: Encouraging Academic Risk-Taking—page 100
- ❖ Tip Sheet 12: Moving Past Perfectionism—page 101
- ❖ Tip Sheet 13: Creating the Ideal Learning Environment—page 104

chapter 10

Leveling the Playing Field

"Teachers and coaches don't get it—they expect everyone to be outgoing and aggressive. And when you aren't, they assume you don't care. It's so wrong."—Bishar, Age 16

The opening quote for this chapter highlights one of the biggest issues introverted children face in our Western culture—the belief that everyone should be outgoing and aggressive in order to get ahead; that somehow success cannot happen without those essential characteristics. As I highlighted in the previous chapter, introverts are not the social or aggressive members of the group. This does not mean they are not motivated. They simply show their commitment in other ways. Hard work and dedication, taking time to help others, intensely listening to coaching, and building connections with a few team members—this is how the introvert demonstrates his commitment to his interests.

In this chapter, I want to focus on the competitive aspects of our culture, building on the interventions in the previous chapter. Children are faced with a higher level of competition than ever before. They are enrolled in more and more extracurricular activities in the name of enrichment. Their academic expectations are rising as well, with an emphasis on high-stakes testing and college preparation. Schools have cut creative arts programs, as well as creative thinking venues. Everything has become goal oriented with reduced emphasis on process. Group collaboration has replaced innovative thinking in education.

Don't get me wrong. The shift in education has developed from a need to improve student achievement and help make our children competitive in a global workforce. But at what price? There are limited opportunities for the introvert to shine in this type of venue.

As I've stated previously, introverts do best when they understand the "why" behind the assignment. They like to experience information in depth and therefore hate to be rushed through tasks. They are innovative and independent in their work efforts. These are skills to be harnessed and developed.

So how can parents help bridge the gap between the current type of expectations placed on introverted thinkers and their natural style of learning? How does the playing field get leveled?

Parents can start by helping their children know what the expectations really are in school. Sit down with them and explain temperament—theirs and the others they may encounter in the room. Help them to understand that neither is better or worse, just different. Once your child understands her temperament in relationship to the school expectations for performance, help your child develop social competency in the areas of initiating conversations with adults and peers, public speaking, and self-advocacy. Taught early and practiced often, these skills, and those on page 109, can help your introverted child be competitive in any environment.

As your child begins to practice and use these social skills, it is imperative that he or she remember to balance out the new and exhausting skills with time to renew. Revisit the healthy habits (page 68) from Chapter 6 and teach your child how to balance the need to be social with the need to renew. This is a balancing act that will need to be frequently

TIP SHEET 14

Social Competency Skills for Introverts

❖ Teach communication skills to your introverted child. Practice initiating conversations.

❖ Help your child practice ways to stay calm and flow with life's ups and downs.

❖ Teach your child to quiet the chatter in his or her head.

❖ Help your child learn to laugh at life.

❖ Build tolerance and flexibility in your introverted child.

reflected upon, as introverted adults and children often struggle with these seemingly opposing motivations. Being on the lookout for signs of frustration and burn-out, including withdrawal and agitation, is a great way to check your child's level of balance.

Academic performance is only one area of competition facing many of our students. Extracurricular areas, including sports and the arts, also include a level of competition for most children. This competitive overlay can be a source of motivation for the extrovert, and something that overwhelms the introvert.

I want to share a story of one child I've worked with in the past. She was a competitive swimmer with Olympic dreams. Starting at age 6, she swam every day. Although very quiet and reserved when her coaches spoke to her, she always listened intently to what they said and incorporated their suggestions into her stroke. She also competed at swim meets, exceeding the goals set by her coaches. On the pool deck, she seldom talked with friends, preferring instead to listen to her iPod and read a book.

One day, her coach decided to move her to a top-level group. She was thrilled. On the day of her first practice at that level, she was sick and barely able to finish the set. Her coach didn't know about the illness and thought she was not ready to move up after all. He suggested that she go back down to her previous group. Unable to explain that she was sick, the swimmer silently nodded and joined the other group.

Her coach never knew that she felt like a failure. He never understood the constant self-talk confirming that she wasn't good enough. He didn't know about the impact of her introversion.

The girl swam for another week before asking her mom if she could quit.

This story highlights some of the realities of introversion. Her inability to talk with her coaches and express her desires and fears, as well as the constant self-talk that replayed her perceived failures over and over again are all aspects of her introversion. Had that been recognized, she could have been coached to respond differently, perhaps with a different outcome. The point is that many times the behavior we see someone engaging in is seldom motivated by the reasons we assume. It is important to understand our children in light of their unique temperament, learning styles, experiences, and personalities.

Sports offer children great opportunities. But they can also be a source of unbearable anxiety. As parents, it is important that you listen to your children and monitor their emotional reactions to the activities they are involved in. Do not be afraid to jump in to coach or support your child if he is struggling at any point with the competition he is experiencing in his extracurricular or educational activities.

How do you jump in to help? What does it mean to be a good emotional coach to your children? I talk a lot about emotional coaching in my book *Emotional Intensity in Gifted Students* (Fonseca, 2010), citing coaching strategies as a great way to assist gifted children in learning how to manage their emotional responses to the world. The same advice bears repeating here, with reference to helping introverted children. Introverted children need to be reminded that there is nothing wrong with their particular view of the world. Yes, they approach things in a different manner from their extroverted counterparts, but this is neither a good nor a bad thing. It is simply a difference in hardwiring.

Being a good coach involves three distinct skills. The first is unconditional high regard. If we want our children to embrace their unique nature, then *we* must. Children need to grow up knowing that no matter how much we understand, or don't understand, their temperament, we accept them exactly as they are. This does not mean we allow inappropriate behavior; it simply means that we love them unconditionally first.

As I discussed in Part II, it is important for our introverted children to have structure, rules, and consequences in the home setting. But we can love them for who they are while we are helping to shape their behavior.

In addition to unconditional high regard, coaching involves good communication and collaboration skills. It is important that parents develop effective communication skills to use with their introverted children. This will not always be easy. Introverts will shy away from direct discussions, especially if the topic is their feelings. They will often resist any conversation that makes them feel like they have failed. If they are already overwhelmed, they will often yell or scream instead of talk. Learning how to work through these roadblocks can be challenging. The tip sheet on page 112 highlights some ways to overcome the more common communication roadblocks. Effective coaching relies on being able to communicate and guide the introvert.

Many times it will feel like your introverted children are not listening. Trust me, regardless of their willingness to openly discuss difficult topics, they are always listening. Don't force a response from your introverted children. Let them listen and take time to process what you are saying. They will come and reengage with you when they are ready. You just need to be available to them when they are.

The last aspect of emotional coaching involves motivation. Effective coaches motivate others to accomplish more than they think possible. As parents, this can be accomplished by encouraging your introverted children to explore their areas of interest and allowing them some freedom to explore these areas at depth. Teach your children how to manage their energy levels, remembering that most introverted children will run low on energy by the evening hours. The more you can encourage their comfort with themselves, the more they can begin to see the strengths of their introversion. That is when they can learn to embrace it and be as competitive as their extroverted peers. Refer back to the tips on page 113 anytime you need to refocus on being an emotional coach to your children.

We live in a competitive global society, taught that the first one up the mountain wins. As adults, we recognize that this is not always the case. Life has a way of reminding us that journeys are at least as important as destinations. Teaching your introverted children to focus on process,

---

TIP SHEET 15

Overcoming Communication Roadblocks

Communication roadblocks can happen from the child and from the parent. Use the tips below to overcome the problems, regardless of how they arise:

- ❖ Overcome whining, yelling, and ignoring forms of communication with these actions:
  - o Remain calm; keep emotions out of the equation.
  - o Clearly and concisely state your desired outcome.
  - o Remind your child of the consequences for good and poor decisions.
  - o Follow through on whatever is decided.

- ❖ Overcome threatening, making judgments, and shaming with these actions:
  - o Use clear and concise language.
  - o Remain emotionally neutral.
  - o Stay focused on your goals.
  - o Don't take the behavior personally.

Remember that introverts struggle with intense emotions. Help maintain communication by remaining calm and focused.

---

embrace their unique temperaments, and balance the need to be competitive and social with the need to renew are all strategies that will prepare them to be the best they can be. And isn't that what we want for our children?

Class Notes: Enhancing, Not Hindering, Performance

Performance and mastery—nowhere is this focus stronger than in today's classrooms. The truth is that we live in a world that measures

TIP SHEET 16

Being a Coach to Your Children

❖ Coaching involves effective communication, teaching, and motivation.

❖ Communication involves understanding the child's needs and wants, active listening, and dealing with roadblocks as they arise.

❖ Teaching involves helping your child understand his or her introversion and focusing on teaching *how* to think, not *what* to think.

❖ Motivation involves having unconditional high regard for your child and being a source of inspiration.

success in terms of performance and skill mastery. Process is not always emphasized the way many educators believe it should be. As has been stated throughout the book, introverts don't always thrive in performance-dominated environments. So how can the teacher maintain the performance quality that is required in our current educational system and enhance, rather than inhibit, the learning of the introvert? Are these two things mutually exclusive?

I believe the answer is a resounding "no." Balancing the educational focus on both mastery and process is the key. By maintaining the balanced approach, more students will be able to demonstrate their talents. Furthermore, differentiation becomes easier as the teacher learns which students are mastery focused and which are process oriented.

Balancing the approach requires using a broad definition of assessment, one that gives credit for both the process of deriving an answer and the answer itself. It also requires a focus on learning for the sake of learning.

Do you allow students to create projects or tasks for some content areas, giving them some flexibility on depth of study? How about exploring unique areas of study within content standards? In today's ever-changing global market, it is even more important that our students learn to think and problem solve. Focusing on both process and result enables this to occur while also providing a venue for the introverted learner to shine.

COMPETITION Q&A

We live in a competitive world. Sports, business, the arts—so much of it is about winning and losing. It isn't surprising, then, that I receive a lot of questions regarding competition and temperament. These questions were pulled from online parent focus questionnaires and my workshops.

Should competitive sports be encouraged for introverted children?

Sports are healthy for kids—all kids. Being involved in sporting activities teaches goal setting, teamwork, discipline, and physical fitness. That said, care should be taken with introverted children when picking the sport. Let your child take the lead and explore a variety of sports before settling in on one or two. If your child is getting stressed in team sports like baseball and soccer, encourage individual sports like swimming or cross country. Likewise, if the attention given during some individual sports overwhelms your child, consider a recreational sport. The key is to find a venue that allows your child to find common interests with peers, while minimizing the potential negative impact of competition and social pressure.

Another positive aspect of competitive sports is the opportunity for physical activity. As I've previously mentioned, introverted children tend to live in their heads, mentally analyzing every aspect of their day. Sports often provide respite to the chatter, allowing both a different type of mental activity and, for many, a break from the mental chatter.

Is there really a downside to competition for introverted children?

Like anything, there are drawbacks to competitive sports for introverted children. Sometimes, the pressure to win can be overwhelming to the introverted child. This can be especially true in team sports. The child may interpret any errors as being his or her fault. But, because of his or her inhibited nature, she may not be able to talk with the coach about it, leaving the feelings to fester and grow. Then there is the issue of risk-taking. As I mentioned earlier, many introverted children struggle with taking academic risks for fear of failure and perfectionism issues. This same hesitancy with academics can extend to any area, in particular competitive team sports. It is important to help your child learn to take risks while also making certain that the competitive environment is not turning toxic to your introverted child.

What skills should introverted children learn to help them deal with our current educational system that focuses on collaboration and group work?

I believe any child benefits from learning basic extrovert skills. Learning to communicate effectively, lessening the mental chatter, and strengthening flexibility are all tools that will enhance the introvert's ability to shine in a group setting. Furthermore, learning to take setbacks in stride and balancing the need to be heard with the need to support the extroverted friend are other skills that will help the introverted child.

As the parent of an introverted high school student, I am worried about the impact of academic competition on my daughter. At the same time, I want her to have every opportunity to get into a great college. Should I be concerned, really?

Academic competition is commonplace on high school campuses now, especially within honors programs. The need to add more and more to the college application, while maintaining a GPA above a 4.0 can drive the most balanced of students into the depths of stress. This is even more true for the introverted child who has not yet learned to deal with stress.

As I mentioned previously, introverted children are naturally self-reflective, often analyzing every minute aspect of their lives. This ability to self-reflect is both an asset and a curse to the child in an honors program. Often, these programs challenge the most academically proficient. And while the challenge is good, it is often accompanied by falling grades. This may be new territory for the child. As an introverted child, he may engage in endless reflection on the failure, getting stuck in a place of stress until he becomes overwhelmed. It is important to help your child achieve the things he wants to achieve without becoming overly stressed.

TIP SHEET 17

Helping Your Students Destress

- ❖ Maintain a safe and calm classroom environment.
- ❖ Teach relaxation techniques and practice them with your class.
- ❖ Encourage preparation as a way to combat test anxiety.
- ❖ Teach test-taking skills.
- ❖ Speak openly about performance-based stress and how to deal with it.
- ❖ If you become concerned about a student, reach out to both the student and the parent.

Teaching him to relax is a great way to put your child in control of his emotional reactions throughout the day. This may help quell the stress inherent in rigorous programs.

I work with many gifted introverted students. What advice do you have for me in helping them deal with highly competitive honors programs in high school?

Similar to the previous question regarding some of the problems introverted children face in rigorous academic programs, this question is all about teaching children to handle the rigor without collapsing under the stress. A teacher is in a unique position to function as a coach for his or her students, teaching both academic and affective content. The tip sheet above is a great list of things you can do in your role as teacher to help your student.

In a Nutshell . . .

Big Ideas

- ❖ We live in a highly competitive world that focuses on results more than process.

❖ Introverts may struggle with results while excelling at process.

❖ It is important for parents and educators to understand some of the difficulties introverts may face.

❖ Introverts can learn social competency skills that help them compete.

❖ Parents can serve a unique role for introverted children by being a "coach" to them, helping them to develop the skills needed to be competitive in sports and school.

❖ Coaching requires unconditional high regard, strong communication skills, and the ability to motivate.

Supplemental Pages

chapter 11

Coping With Failure

"I never share my grades, even when they are good. It's just too personal."—Maya, Age 13

As competition and rigor increase in schools, so does the possibility for failure. As discussed in Chapter 9, introverted children struggle with taking academic risks. This is often related to the failure that is always possible when taking risks, as well as some problems with resiliency.

In Chapter 6, resiliency was defined as the ability to recover or adjust to change. Clearly taking appropriate risks is at least partially related to the ability or willingness to recover from setbacks. When students take risks in competition, they allow for the possibility of failure. Resilient children understand that such possibility just comes with the territory. Children who may struggle with some aspect of resiliency see the risk as unnecessary and guard against it at all costs, even when that means forgoing certain goals.

I remember when my daughter was in band, she was second chair in the flute section. When I asked why she didn't challenge for first chair, she stated that she could fail. When I pushed a little harder to know how she was defining failure, she diverted the conversation, stating instead that she really didn't "need" to be first chair; that it was more important to her friend to remain in that position. Now, I don't doubt that her friend's needs factored into my daughter's decisions. But I also know that she is not a risk taker. When presented with taking a risk and meeting her own needs, or maintaining the status quo and meeting a friend's needs, the latter was a clear choice.

My daughter's rationale is a typical example of how introverts weigh their options. It also points to the incessant thinking that comes with nearly every decision. Introverted children consider and ponder everything. Their minds are constantly chatting, providing rationale for everything that happens. As I've stated previously, sometimes this is good, allowing the introvert to delve more deeply into things as compared with the extroverted child. However, many times introverts go too far, allowing their thinking to trap them in indecision. They weigh every option ad nauseam; afraid to make any one decision for fear that it is the wrong decision. Their resiliency is challenged as they sacrifice mastery in order to prevent mistakes. It is a never-ending trap that moves the introverted child closer to inaction and the resultant failure.

In other words, it is the exact opposite of what they should do to combat their fear of failure.

Parents can help introverted children in this predicament by reinforcing both the resiliency skills previously discussed, and pointing out the connection between failure and inaction. Developing autonomy over situations, as well as having a strong support system and balancing emotional reactions are all components of resiliency that can combat any negative effects of failure, real or perceived. But resiliency alone may not be enough. Introverted children may also need to reframe their definition of failure.

In today's world, events are often framed in rigid terms. You can be either right or wrong. Things are either good or bad. In reality, nothing is that black and white. Most of us function in a world comprised of a

TIP SHEET 18
Building Tolerance for Change

- ❖ Help your child identify his or her concerns regarding change.
- ❖ Teach problem-solving skills.
- ❖ Be a role model for flexibility.
- ❖ Incorporate opportunities for unplanned change into the week.
- ❖ Teach that "change" is normal and point out change within the environment.

million shades of gray, one in which the only guaranteed road to dissatisfaction is stagnation.

Introverted children are highly resistant to change. They would rather suffer through an unpleasant situation than risk taking action and having a worse scenario. They seldom realize that the natural order of things is action. So inaction is actually the thing to be avoided. Sure, taking any action involves a measure of risk and the potential of at least perceived failure. But if we can assist our introverted children in developing a tolerance for some amount of change, as well as helping them realize that change is one of the few guarantees in this world, we go a long way to increasing their capacity to cope with perceived failure. The tips on page 121 give several suggestions for increasing your introverted child's tolerance for change and decreasing the rigidity that typically accompanies this type of temperament.

It's important to note that the more overwhelmed the introverted child becomes, the more rigid he or she may appear. Take time to notice the ebb and flow of your child's moods and try to coach your child prior to the stress grabbing hold. Revisit the healthy lifestyle choices discussed in Chapter 6. Making sure that your introverted child is eating appropriately, getting plenty of rest, and taking time to renew his or her energy stores is critical in preventing many of the negative aspects of stress and poor coping skills. Once your child becomes entrenched in her rigidity, you will have a more difficult time coaxing her into some sort of action.

TIP SHEET 19

Recovering From Setbacks

❖ Detach from the immediate crisis.

❖ Take a moment to calm yourself. Remind your child how to calm him- or herself.

❖ Debrief from the outburst once everyone is out of the crisis.

❖ Give your child space and time to decompress.

❖ Reevaluate your child's schedule to prevent future energy overloads.

Sometimes, despite our best efforts, our introverted children experience failure and loss in ways that overwhelm their system. They withdraw, become belligerent and shut down. Now the focus for parents needs to be on recovery. This will be difficult much of the time, as the anger and frustration felt by the introverted child is often aimed right at the parents. Remembering to not take things personally and focusing on helping the child get back to a state of calm may take all of your strength. In fact, I am certain it will. But engaging in a battle when your introverted child is in this state is a useless endeavor that will only end in misery for everyone involved. Instead, take a step back and help your child regain control over his or her emotions. Use the Managing My Reactions tips (see page 52) from Chapter 5 to help you stay detached. Pull on the relaxation strategies found in Relaxation 101 (see page 80) outlined in Chapter 7 and help your child find his center again. When the crisis is over and your child is calm, then you can enter into a conversation about avoiding the crisis in the future. Remember that overwhelmed introverts will become even less verbal and less able to problem solve. Give them the time and space they need to decompress prior to trying to redirect their behavior. Recovering from setbacks is a vital aspect of resiliency, and one that parents can help develop in their children. The tip sheet on this page bullets the things to consider when teaching children how to bounce back from life's misfortunes.

No chapter focused on coping with failure would be complete without mentioning gifted children, and gifted introverts in particular. Gifted children are a naturally intense group that tends to be more introverted than other groups (Sword, 2000). Given the natural hardwiring of introverts, I am not surprised that an introverted temperament is more prevalent amongst gifted children. Gifted introverts have the same need as all introverts—solitude. However, they present the more negative aspects of introversion at more intense levels. When they pull away from the hectic environment at school and disappear into a book, they often appear to have completely withdrawn from social interactions. When they become overwhelmed, they typically become explosive related to their giftedness and the inherent intensities. This explosive nature often results in misdiagnoses and mistreatment by well-meaning parents and professionals who do not understand that explosive behavior to an overwhelmed introverted gifted child is "normal."

Helping the gifted child is similar to helping any introverted child, but at a comparably more intense level. With gifted children, it is imperative to address the concerns earlier rather than later. Help these children develop healthy lifestyle choices, balance their overscheduled lives and become very aware of their introversion. In this way, you can give the gifted introvert the ability to take control of his choices and learn to balance his introversion earlier, rather than later.

Class Notes: Maintaining a Healthy Perspective About Failure

Failure is something most educators are faced with on a daily basis as children learn and gain mastery over ever increasingly difficult skills. But dealing with the introverted student's experience with failure may be a little trickier than you realize. Consider this common scenario: You are passing out graded papers. The extroverts are looking at their grades and sharing their opinions on them with most of their friends. Not the introverts. They are putting their paper aside after stealing a quick glance. If they have earned the grade they expected, then there is no problem. However, if the grade is lower than expected or if they have failed, then a host of emotions happen at once. First, they likely engage in a series of self-deprecating remarks. Then, they likely engage in a little fantasizing about what their parents will think or what the grade may mean for their future. Then the frustration sets in as their senses get overwhelmed by their internal emotional responses. This entire chain happens undetected by the teacher or the other students. No one realizes that the child has just run through an emotional crisis. If the introverted child has a particularly well-developed public mask, he or she is able to continue in the class and even the rest of the day without anyone seeing the turmoil brewing just under the surface. If the mask is not yet well-developed, then the student may ask to see the nurse because of a headache, or go to the bathroom to cry—anywhere but in a public venue.

The teacher may never know what the student was feeling about the failure he or she just experienced. In fact, the teacher may think the student doesn't care about the grade or that the child has amazing resiliency skills and is very well-adjusted. It isn't until the child has a huge behavioral explosion outside of class or at home that anyone knows there was a problem.

So what can you do to help the child process the grade without becoming overwhelmed by perceived failure? First, start the year by valuing both mastery and process, as I've stated elsewhere. Teach your students that learning only happens through risk and failure. Once you've established a balanced approach to teaching, focus on knowing your students. Go back to Part I and make sure you know which of your students are introverts. When they receive a grade that is low, give them time to process it. Approach them if you want them to retake a test or discuss the grade. Don't wait for them to speak with you. If you have concerns about their behavior, make certain to connect with their parents. Work as partners to help the introverted child learn that failure is a natural part of learning. Guiding your student to a less rigid view of success and failure is the best way to ensure that all learners, especially introverted learners, maintain a healthy perspective when it comes to grades and performance.

PRESSURE TO PERFORM Q & A

Children are under a lot of pressure to perform in today's schools. Expectations around state and national testing, competition in sports and academics, as well as pressure to "make the grade" can hinder our children's achievement, especially that of our introverted children. The questions below have come from parents and teachers when discussing their feelings about statewide testing throughout the U.S., and the pressures they see in their children.

My son is having major problems on math tests. He knows the material at home but cannot translate that into test taking. He also has issues focusing in math class. But he insists that math is his favorite subject. What are some ways we can help him with his school performance?

My guess is that math *is* his favorite subject, regardless in his performance in this area. It is important to remember that performance in a subject doesn't correlate to enjoyment. There are plenty of things I enjoy but do not excel at. All of that said, there are things you can do to help him with his performance on math tests. First, make sure he has had ample time to prepare for the tests. Spread the studying out over several days. Second, change the focus from performance to process. In other words, focus on how he is learning the material, not his accuracy levels. There is a possibility that he is "choking" on tests related to performance pressure. Finally, watch out for overstudying. Yes, that's right, you can be too prepared for a test. As I've previously discussed, introverts engage in high levels of self-talk, often narrating their day and, more importantly, their feelings about the day. When a student is experiencing difficulties in performance in a specific area, the chatter may be undermining confidence by restating past failures in an endless loop. Take some time to help your child learn to discern his mental chatter and change any negation to positive, empowering talk. Use some of the strategies discussed in the chatter to help your child script more positive mental discourse. It will take practice, but it will help.

Are there programs in place to help these types of kids? What steps can parents take to get their introverted kids help if they are struggling?

Schools have gotten much better at addressing academic difficulties with children. The recent Response to Intervention (RtI) movement has provided a framework to address academic remediation in the general education setting. This framework for interventions is designed to be available to any child at any time during his or her academic career. With introverts, however, the apparent academic difficulties may be rooted in something other than an actual deficit in skill mastery. It could be rooted in the very nature of introversion. If the child is struggling with oral presentations or fast-paced quizzes, the introversion may be hindering her ability to demonstrate mastery. In these cases it is important to understand the root cause of the difficulty before developing an action plan. Once the cause has been determined, the parent and school can partner to develop a solution. The tip sheet on page 127 highlights some considerations for the team as a plan is developed.

How can I help my school officials to understand what introversion really is?

As I have stated in previous Q&As, most teacher preparation programs do not teach educators about the impact of temperament on learning. Your child's teacher may not understand that the difficulties the child is having is related to introversion or that there are no real difficulties at all—just a difference in learning style. It is important for parents, as the primary advocate for your child, to work with the school regarding your child. Set up a meeting with the teacher early in the year and provide him or her with information about your child's unique learning and temperament styles. Then, as things surface throughout the year, work in partnership with the school to ensure that your child is getting an appropriate education. Finally, remember that while the educators are experts in teaching, you are the expert on your child. Working collaboratively with the school enables all parties to form an alliance to help the child.

TIP SHEET 20

Developing a Plan

- ❖ Establish mutual goals for meetings and the plan.
- ❖ Discuss strengths of the child before looking at the concerns.
- ❖ Problem solve those areas of difficulty the child is experiencing.
- ❖ Decide on measureable goals to focus on.
- ❖ Keep it simple.
- ❖ Revisit the plan often to monitor progress.
- ❖ Rework the plan as needed.

My daughter seems to get caught in a loop of negative thinking. Is there something I can do to help her change this kind of thinking?

Ah yes, the loop of doom. I know it well. Most introverts get stuck in this loop from time to time, hyperfocusing on past failures and other forms of negation. Helping your daughter change her thinking starts with helping her be aware of her thought patterns to begin with. Use the worksheets and tips throughout this chapter to help her identify the types of negation she engages in, replacing her thoughts with more positive messages. Also, help her establish time in her day when she can turn off her thoughts all together. Meditation, sports, and even types of creative endeavors can help her with this. Learning to control the never-ending thinking inherent in introversion is vital to her developing a more balanced temperament.

I think some of my students have been misidentified as disabled in some way when maybe it is more a matter of temperament. Is it possible for that to happen?

Yes, students can get mislabeled when the real issue involves temperament. Many times Attention Deficit/Hyperactivity Disorder (ADHD) labels are given to both extroverted and introverted children related to apparent hyperactivity in the former group, and assumed inattention in the later group. Likewise, diagnoses of autism spectrum disorder (ASD), sensory integration disorder, and anxiety disorders can often be mislabeling of introversion. I believe this happens because many of these diagnoses are rule-out diagnoses with large behavioral components. These behaviors can mimic one another, causing some difficulties with doing a differential diagnosis. It is important that any labels, educational or medical, be given by qualified personnel who are well-trained in multiple areas and making difficult differential diagnoses. In the school setting, where labels are placed based on students' behaviors consistent with various diagnoses and needs, it is especially important that school psychologists and other personnel are careful not to mislabel, and therefore mistreat, students.

Although it is not uncommon to mislabel students who are introverted as something more significant, it is also possible to be both introverted and anxious or introverted and a student with ASD. Temperament alone does not preclude these possibilities. The key is making sure to keep the whole child in mind when assigning the labels or recommending certain diagnoses.

In a Nutshell . . .

Big Ideas

❖ Developing good coping skills to deal with failure involves developing strong resiliency skills.

❖ Introverts often battle with failure related to:
  o the internal "thinking" trap,
  o struggling between the needs of others and their own needs, and
  o the struggle between their public and private personas.

❖ Change is the natural order of things.

❖ Introverts struggle with change and may need help to develop a tolerance for change.

❖ Introverts can become explosive when faced with failure.

❖ Gifted introverts have similar needs and difficulties to other introverts, but react in ways that are even more intense.

Supplemental Pages

chapter 12

In Their Own Words

The Pressure to Succeed— High School Introverts Speak Out

I started running focus groups when I was researching my two self-help books for kids, *101 Success Secrets for Gifted Kids* and *The Girl Guide*. I met with hundreds of kids, asking them specific questions about everything from giftedness, to school, to peer pressure and more.

One of the focus groups with high schoolers covered the ideas of temperament and the pressure to perform in honors-level classes. I've taken some of the content from that group and included it here. It speaks to the pressures many bright introverted teens feel when it comes to meeting the expectations of a world that celebrates extroversion, sometimes at the expense of introversion.

Before I jump into the actual interview, let me give you a few demographics for the group. The participation group for these questions consisted of 11 high school juniors and seniors (five boys and six girls). Ethnicity was diverse, consisting of Asian, Pacific Islander, African American, Hispanic, and White. Socioeconomic levels were unknown. Each of the participants had been identified at their school as being gifted. They self-identified themselves as being introverted based on their preference for solitude when they needed to renew. Nine participants were involved in their honors programs (five girls and four boys), while the other two took at least one honors-level class during their high school career. All 11 participants were involved in at least one extracurricular activity, with nine participants being involved in three or more activities during the school year. All participants stated that they planned to apply for a 4-year college. Group participants were not obligated to provide their names. For that reason, I have identified them as Students 1 through 11.

I want to thank you all, again, for participating in this evening's group. The following questions involve what it means to be introverted in today's academically challenging world. Let's start with a basic question—Do you think school is harder for an introvert?

Student 1: I do, totally.

Student 8: I think our teachers always expect that we have time to do the projects and papers. And that's on top of the extracurricular things we are expected to participate in.

Student 11: There is just a lot of pressure to get "out there," get known. For me, it's really uncomfortable.

Student 1: Yeah, I would prefer to stay behind the scenes, you know? But that doesn't get you noticed by colleges.

Student 3: Some of our teachers just expect us to have no problem with speaking in front of class and actively participating in the interactive circles [Socratic seminars]. It's hard for me.

Student 11: At least we have each other, though.

Student 3: That's what gets me through it all, knowing my friends "get" me and are going through the same thing.

What about the pressure to excel? Is there a difference in how that pressure is felt based on temperament?

Student 2: That's a hard question to answer. I am an introvert. I've got no idea how my extroverted friends feel. It isn't something we ever talk about.

Student 6: I will say that most of my extroverted friends are more vocal about the pressure, that's for sure.

(*Laughter and nods from the group.*)

Student 6: Seriously, I have friends that seem more outgoing than I am. They talk about feeling a lot of pressure at school. In fact, they talk about it frequently.

Student 3: But not us. I think the only time I ever talk about the pressures I'm feeling is if someone else brings it up. And even then, I am hesitant to admit what I am feeling. I won't even tell my mom about how I feel most of the time. It's just too hard.

Is that true for most of you? Are you hesitant to ever talk about your stress and pressure?

(*More nodding.*)

Student 10: I think that all of us in honors programs feel a lot of pressure to excel. It kind of goes along with the territory. We need to get good grades, participate in leadership activities, be in sports or artistic groups, volunteer places. It is a lot to handle. But I don't think that is unique to introverts. Everyone in these types of programs is going to feel some level of pressure. I just think introverted kids talk about it less.

Are any of you involved in competitive sports? Is it hard, given your temperament?

Student 5: We aren't all involved in sports, I think. But we are in competitive activities.

Student 6: Mock trial, debate, sports. Something that will look good on the college application.

Student 5: Yeah. And we all try to have leadership roles in those groups. That is the hardest part for me. If one of my more outgoing friends wants the same position, I will seldom go for it. Instead, I'll create some new position that I can have. It's just easier than trying to "sell" myself to the other people in the group.

Student 3: I'm a competitive swimmer. It's not hard for me to be in the group at all. I just swim, listen to music in between events at a meet, and chill. No big deal.

Student 11: I'm in swim too. And yeah, it isn't really hard in terms of my temperament or anything. Though, I have to admit, my coaches don't get the whole introvert thing. They don't get that yelling at me in front of everyone is rough on me.

Student 7: Yeah, coaches never seem to care about how being corrected loudly on the field feels.

What about other extracurricular activities? Are you more drawn to certain types? What are they?

Student 2: I think our interests are diverse, just like everything else. Sure, many of us are involved in similar things. But I think that is more related to our college goals. We are all drawn to the activities that look the best on college applications.

Student 5: Some of us like mock trial or debate. Some of us are more drawn to service or religious-based groups. And others are into the arts.

Student 2: We just all try to be involved in a lot of different things. For college.

Student 9: Not just for college. I like being involved in speech. It has helped me overcome some of my fear of public speaking.

Do you think it is harder for an introvert to get into college? Why or why not?

Student 1: I don't think temperament has anything to do with getting into college.

Student 3: Except for the interview part. I know I'm scared of that piece.

Student 1: Yeah, but everyone is afraid of that part! And besides, we have classes we can take to prepare for that.

Student 3: Yeah, classes that make us role-play. That's almost as bad as the interview itself.

Student 9: I'm not worried about getting into college. And I don't think temperament has anything to do with entrance. But I think I'm more drawn to small colleges related to my temperament. The idea of 50 or 100 in a class sounds horrible to me. My short-list for colleges have ratios more like 10-1.

What is the biggest challenge in high school for an introvert?

Students 4 and 5: The social drama.

Student 5: I just hate having to deal with the social aspects of high school. I do feel lucky to have found a bunch of people that understand my moods, my need to be alone, and my unwillingness to talk about some things. But it is really hard with some of my other classmates.

Student 9: I just feel like I am misunderstood a lot. Even by my friends. They think that I am being, I don't know, a snob I guess. They just don't get my need to be alone, or my hesitancy in groups.

Student 5: We get you!

Student 9: I know you do, but there are a lot of people who don't. They assume I'm being conceited when I pull away. Or that there is something "wrong" with me. I think that's the hardest part of high school.

Student 10: I get that. And I have to say that I agree—the social part just sucks most of the time. It's taken me 3 years to find friends that are like me. This year has been a lot better because of it. Next year, since we are all going to different schools and such, I'm a little nervous. I don't want to go back to feeling like I'm totally alone again.

For you seniors, will some of you try to stay in touch?

Student 10: I know I will—on Facebook or by texting.

Student 5: Yeah, I definitely plan on staying in touch with everyone.

This glimpse into the minds of a group of gifted introverts provided me with a lot of insight into some of the things they find more difficult as an introvert trying to make it in an extroverted culture. Their responses shaped some of the strategies developed for the book. I hope you find their insights helpful as you deepen you understanding and develop your own strategies for working with your introverted children.

Introverted Kids at Play

Social dynamics are challenging for introverts. This section examines social dynamics and the introvert, including tips related to developing social skills and helping the child discover her unique place in the world.

Western culture often measures social success in terms of the number of friends you have, your ability to interact in social situations, and your ability to "sell" yourself in any given situation. For the introverted child, trying to live up to these ideas may be an act of futility. Parents often feel like a failure when their introverted child is unable to cope with the social pressures placed by a culture that negates the real needs of the introvert.

This section looks at social dynamics and the introverted child, examining the pressures to interact socially and the ways introverted children can connect without sacrificing their need for solitude. Development of strong social resiliency, as well as ways in which technology can enhance the introvert's ability to connect are also examined. The section ends with advice for parents on assisting their children in embracing their strengths and thriving in an overwhelming world.

As we begin this section of the book, I want you to reflect on your feelings about social dynamics and the pressure to fit in. Take a couple of minutes to answer the questions on page 139 before you read the upcoming chapters.

QUESTIONNAIRE 5

Ideas About Social Dynamics and the Introvert

1. My introverted child does well socially in terms of . . . (*complete the sentence*).

2. My introverted child struggles socially in terms of . . . (*complete the sentence*).

3. My biggest concern for my introverted child socially is . . . (*complete the sentence*).

4. I wish my introverted child was more outgoing. *True or False*
   ❑ *True*   ❑ *False*

5. My introverted child has a strong sense of self. *True or False*
   ❑ *True*   ❑ *False*

6. If I answered "false" above, I think the biggest obstacle is . . . (*complete the sentence*).

Once you are finished, take a moment to reflect on your answers and consider the following questions: What is your biggest worry when it comes to your child and his or her social development? What is your child's best strength in terms of social development? What is his or her biggest obstacle?

chapter 13

Surviving the Social Scene

"I know what I have to do to fit in. It's hard, but being considered an outcast is even harder."—Pedro, Age 12

Social development can be hard for most children as the push and pull between needs and expectations gets increasingly harder to navigate. This is particularly true with introverts who are often misperceived by the dominant, extroverted culture.

Western society has given the message that you must be socially aggressive in order to be heard. And those who are heard get further than those who are not. Little influence is given to those who are more reserved or quiet, despite their accomplishments. Furthermore, people are often praised for their ability to gain large numbers of friends and participate in highly social venues, while those who are more socially withdrawn are given labels suggesting that they are somehow "less" for being so. Despite recent acknowledgement of the power of introversion through books like *Quiet* by Susan Cain and similar publications, if you Google "introvert," then you will still get a disproportionally high amount of entries that define it in negative terms.

So how are introverts perceived by their extroverted counterparts, and what is the impact on social development? Most people see introverted children as shy, withdrawn, or aloof. They are characterized as being too self-absorbed, loners, or with other derogatory terms. These characterizations leave introverted children feeling like they are damaged somehow. They begin to believe that unless they can overcome their hesitancy to develop an outgoing personality, then they will forever be doomed to being slightly less than their more social peers.

Obviously, this is the extreme version of what many introverts feel. But it is something we need to consider as we assist our introverted children in becoming adults.

Introverted children actually have a lot to offer friendships. Deeply interested in the world and in learning, introverts have the potential to develop relationships at a much deeper level as compared to their extroverted counterparts. Furthermore, many introverted adults are neither shy nor aloof. I am a great example of this. As I mentioned in the beginning of the book, I am very comfortable presenting to hundreds of people. But keep me in such a large crowd for too long, and my energy becomes dangerously depleted. I am deeply passionate about my interests, often working longer than many of my extroverted friends. I am able to connect and maintain several friendships and have little difficulty articulating my needs and wants. Granted, these are skills I have spent a lifetime learning, but it is all proof that the early misperceptions of my introversion did not have to result in a permanent problem.

So how is the gulf between what introverts are perceived to be and what they can become bridged? I think it starts with helping our introverted children see the strengths in their introversion, not just the negative messages they may receive on a daily basis. This can happen by working with them to focus on the strengths of their temperament. Go back to Chapter 3 and rework through the worksheet The Positive Aspects of My Introversion (see p. 36). Help your child make a list of these positive statements that she can regularly refer to in order to remind herself of her strengths.

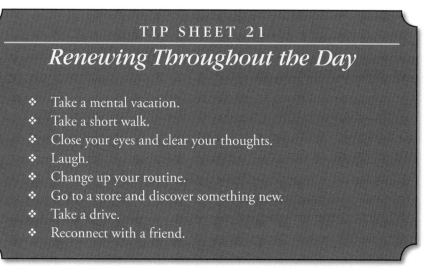

In addition to focusing on strengths, it is important that your introverted children understand the possible downside of their introversion. Remind them of the reality of their energy levels and how they need to renew. Help refine the healthy habits they have previously established in order to maintain their healthy habits. And help them recognize the aspects of their day that can function as energy zappers.

Knowing what types of things drain your introverted children is the first step in developing a plan to combat the fatigue. The tips offered on this page give several examples of ways to quickly renew when the introvert's energy is on the decline.

Becoming comfortable with introversion isn't always enough. Sometimes the best gift we can give our introverts is to develop social competencies that enable them to function more as an extrovert when required. I remember working with a family on this issue. Their son enjoyed participating in drama. Although he had no difficulties during the actual production, acting his part in front of an audience with ease, he struggled with rehearsals. The hours and the constant social interactions left him drained to the point of frustration, often resulting in outbursts at home. Through our work, we discovered that he never felt "heard" during rehearsals. He would give suggestions once or twice, but usually gave up when he felt like he couldn't get a word in over the loud utterances of his very extroverted coactor. His parents and I worked on

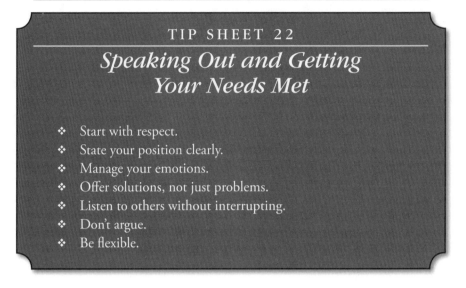

TIP SHEET 22

Speaking Out and Getting Your Needs Met

❖ Start with respect.

❖ State your position clearly.

❖ Manage your emotions.

❖ Offer solutions, not just problems.

❖ Listen to others without interrupting.

❖ Don't argue.

❖ Be flexible.

helping him advocate for himself and articulate his needs. We started with speaking only to one or two people, working up to being able to make suggestions in front of a large group. The tips above highlight some ways to help your introverted child learn to self-advocate when needed.

We also worked on ways to renew his energy during rehearsals. Between the two things, the young man learned how to make the most of his experiences in drama, without some of the more negative issues.

Some of the social skills necessary to survive in our culture include the ability to be heard within the crowd, the ability to be seen within the crowd, the art of conversation, and the ability to collaborate within a group. These skills, while difficult for the introvert to initially learn, can make a large positive impact in the introvert's ability to function in our Western culture. Furthermore, learning these skills while also learning to regulate one's energy will enable the introvert to meet his or her goals within our current society.

Figure 7 builds on the social competency skills listed in Chapter 10, including both the obstacles many introverts face when acquiring these skills and a few tricks for overcoming them. Use it as a place to start with your introverted child, focusing on the easiest to acquire skills first.

Acquiring a collection of extroverted social skills does not mean there is something wrong with being an introvert, far from it. It simply means that in order to enhance the strengths of introversion, certain social com-

Skill	Potential Obstacles	Solutions
Conversation Skills	Initiating conversations	Practice with friends
Relaxation	Difficult when overwhelmed	Practice the skill when not stressed
Flexibility	Introverts crave routine and structure in order to feel safe	Incorporate spontaneity into the daily routine; teach problem-solving skills
Inner Stillness	Introverts constantly think through their day	Include periods of stillness or meditation into the daily routine
Humor	Introverts can be very serious	Seek out opportunities to laugh

Figure 7. Social competency skills revisited.

petencies are required. And these include many of the skills innately possessed by extroverted children.

As introverts begin to become more social, there may be a tendency to overdo it, losing themselves and their introverted voice in the noisy world of extroverts. It is important to emphasize balance during this time. Too many social outings, too much time spent in noisy settings with many people, and too much emphasis on external socializing will exhaust the introvert. And as I've stated multiple times, energy drains almost always guarantee behavioral challenges down the road as the introvert rebels against the drain, becoming belligerent and frustrated. Be mindful of your introverted children. Pay attention to their moods as they begin to experiment socially. Help them renew when they forget to take time for themselves.

No conversation about social interactions and introverted children would be complete without addressing the issue of friendships. Many parents spend a lot of time worried about peer interactions. "Do my children have enough friends? Are they skilled socially for the world at large?" These and other questions flood my inbox with amazing regularity. In my opinion, the question is never "Does my child have enough friends?", but rather "Are my child's friends *close* friends? Is my child enhanced by the relationship in some way?"

We have all had the experience of a friendship that was a drain on our lives, not enhancing it in some way. This can happen with children too. Extroverts seldom stress over these interactions, moving carefree from relationship to relationship with ease. Introverts, however, may struggle with friendships. As stated earlier, introverted children develop deep connections built on intimacy. They are interested in the inner workings of others. Because of this, they only form a few friendships at a time. And if those friendships fade, which typically happens throughout childhood, introverted children may struggle with their emotional reaction to the loss.

It's important for parents to encourage introverts to make friendships, understanding that one or two are plenty. It is also important that parents help their introverted children understand that relationships may come and go throughout a lifetime. This is normal and not something to be taken too much to heart. Knowing the introvert, he or she will engage in a mental analysis with each and every encounter, especially if they fade away unexpectedly.

Parents can play a pivotal role in helping their introverts learn to quell that inner dialogue and balance the emotional reaction. Focusing on seeing life as something that is constantly changing is one way to help introverted children understand the transient nature of childhood friendships. Introverts, as I've mentioned before, don't like change much, but learning that life is ever-changing can help prepare them for the changes that happen in social domains throughout childhood.

Overall, introverted children have great things to offer socially. Like most things, they approach friendships from a different point of view than many of their extroverted counterparts. And although learning a few critical social skills will enhance their social experiences, their innate ability to form deep connections is something that is to be developed and celebrated.

Class Notes: Nurturing Self-Esteem for Educators

Most educators are keenly aware of the impact of esteem and motivation on learning. And teachers are always looking for ways to nurture and enhance these attributes within the classroom setting. This can be particularly important with several subsets of students, including introverted learners.

As I've discussed in Section III, some classroom environments work against the abilities of the introvert, challenging the development of their self-esteem and overall resiliency. But there are things educators can do right now to improve the outcomes for these students and nurture the development of healthy self-esteem and self-efficacy.

It begins with understanding the various temperaments in the classroom and the impact of this on overall performance, something I have already discussed at length. Once there is a good foundation of understanding, educators can focus on building connections with students. This is particularly helpful with introverted students who require deeper levels of connection in order to feel safe. Remembering to use performance-based praise, given both individually and in a larger group format is another way in which educators can build a classroom that nurtures the self-esteem of students. It's important that this praise be given more frequently than corrections, and that it is specific for the child. Praise for the sake of praise has been repeatedly found to be ineffective in motivating or nurturing children. So link the praise to performance and/or behavior. For introverted learners, be sure to deliver that praise individually, not just in groups where the attention may negate the positive impact of the words.

Classroom discipline and structure is another important area of consideration when teaching introverted students. As stated previously, introverts thrive on structure, awareness of expectations, and routines. That said, they will cower when the learning environment is negative. They do not respond well to loud or intense voices, nor do they respond to public correction. All of this feels like humiliation to the introverted learner, something she has little tolerance for. Instead, save corrections for private moments with children. Monitor your own emotional status to ensure that you are not inadvertently making the classroom overly harsh or intense. Maintain a calm environment as much as possible.

Finally, look at your mix of students. Do you have some who dominate conversations or engage in relational aggression? Do other students shy away and withdraw in your class? These could be indicators that the room is not as nurturing as you may intend. Use these types of behavioral clues as indicators of the need for balance and seek ways to more strongly meet the needs of your whole class. Doing so will make your classroom a nurturing place for all learners. Refer to the tips on page 149 for ways to keep your classroom a nurturing environment conducive to learning for all students.

SOCIAL DYNAMICS Q&A

One of the areas parents regularly express concerns about is related to social development. Does my child have enough friends? Will she be able to function out in the world?—these are questions that seem to be at the forefront of most parents' thoughts.

I collected several of these questions from workshops and my online focus groups and condensed them into the five questions listed below. I hope they provide additional insight into specific ways we can nurture and support our introverted children's social development.

It seems like my daughter never has friends. Is this true of most introverts?

Parents often worry about the number of friends their children have, and how often they are interacting with their friends. It is a natural area of concern. That said, it is important to recognize that many introverted children need "alone time" more than they need interaction time with friends. After being around large groups of people for 6 or 7 hours every day in school, they may need time to renew in solitude. Don't mistake this withdrawal for not having friends. More often than not, introverted

---

TIP SHEET 23

The Nurturing Classroom

- ❖ Build a safe environment that encourages academic risk-taking.
- ❖ Know the temperaments of your students.
- ❖ Build connections with students.
- ❖ Focus on process first, mastery second.
- ❖ Be consistent with expectations and behavior management.
- ❖ Give performance-based feedback frequently.
- ❖ Deal with bullying and aggression quickly.

---

children have a few close friends that they can rely on. Introverts are all about building close relationships, so the friendships they forge are usually very deep. But, after a busy day, or a difficult week, your introverted children may decide to spend a few days in solitude. This is nothing to be alarmed about.

Ask your child to tell you about his or her friends. Listen for mentions of names as your child recounts his or her day. Odds are good that your child has at least one close friend.

How can introverts and extroverts get on the "same page" with their interactions?

Introverts and extroverts sometimes struggle as they try to interact, misunderstanding each other's intentions. Finding common ground can be difficult. But the truth is, both offer something the other needs. Introverts offer their extroverted peers a chance to develop a deep relationship, as well as an example of how to slow down and contemplate life more. Extroverts offer introverts opportunities for action. Never comfortable with stagnation, extroverts teach introverts to think less, get out of their heads, and enjoy life.

In order for introverts and extroverts to reap the benefits of a relationship with one another, it is important that both temperaments understand each other, including how they can be misperceived. In doing this, they can develop awareness of each others' needs and forge mutually beneficial friendships. As parents, you are in a great position to teach both introverts and extroverts about each other and monitor the early stages of their relationships, guiding them to a deeper understanding about each other.

How can I help others understand that my introverted child isn't "just shy," he actually "sees" the world differently?

Similar to previously asked questions about talking with teachers about introversion, this question really speaks to the need to help others in understanding the ins and outs of temperament. The figures and lists presented in Part I can assist parents in pinpointing the nuances of introversion and provide the information needed when explaining the characteristics of introversion to others. Reminding family members and others that shyness is a behavior that can be shaped, while introversion relates to the brain's hardwiring, is a great way of explaining the basis of temperament.

You've mentioned "extroverted" skills that really help introverted children. Can you tell me a little more about these skills and how to help my child?

Everyone, most especially introverts, need social competency skills—the ability to feel comfortable within social settings and converse with many different types of people. Extroverts can do this naturally, feeding off of the collective energy of a group. Introverts, however, find such social venues exhausting in the best of scenarios, often struggling to initiate casual conversations within a group or initiating any conversation at all.

Parents can help their introverted children by teaching them how to get their needs met and interact in a group at a young age. Encourage them to order their own meal at a restaurant, for example. Or help them to tolerate group activities by providing opportunities to gather with friends for a game night or craft.

It is important that parents take care not to overstimulate or overstress their introverted children by trying to build these skills too quickly. Most introverted children will struggle with both initiating conversations and participating in groups. Teach your children how to monitor their energy levels to prevent burn-out, and speak openly about the strengths and downsides of introversion. All of this will help you raise well-balanced children, capable of functioning in a milieu of social situations.

As an educator, I see my introverted students struggling on the playground. What can I do to help them with their social competencies?

As with all areas of education, I think balance is the key when dealing with introverted children. It is important that introverts be given opportunities for renewal at school, while also developing their social skills. Rather than allow them to withdraw completely from social dynamics, provide some respite from the playground, like being able to go to the library or a classroom, but encourage them to bring a friend or two. In this way, the introverts can develop social competencies while also getting the break they need. Taking the time to seek creative solutions to some of the problems facing our introverted children allows educators to find the win-win solution that benefits all of the introverted student's needs.

In a Nutshell . . .

Big Ideas

❖ Introverts have the capacity to develop strong social skills.

❖ Introverts focus on deep connections with a few, rather than many, friendships.

❖ Oftentimes, introverts are misunderstood by the dominant culture, typically seen as shy, aloof, or socially inept.

❖ Learning a few survival social skills can help introverts overcome the misperceptions. These skills include learning how to stand out in a crowd, the art of conversations, and working collaboratively.

❖ Introverts become drained from too much social contact. It's important for them to learn which types of things present the largest pull to their energy levels.

❖ Parents can play a pivotal role in helping introverted children balance their needs related to their introversion and their need to connect socially.

Supplemental Pages

❖ Tip Sheet 21: Renewing Throughout the Day—page 143
❖ Tip Sheet 22: Speaking Out and Getting Your Needs Met—page 144
❖ Figure 7: Social Competency Skills Revisited—page 145
❖ Tip Sheet 23: The Nurturing Classroom—page 149

chapter 14

Navigating Through the Mine Fields

"Yes, I've been teased because I am so quiet. I hated it. But most people just don't get me."—Daniel, Age 8

Social venues can be difficult for any child, especially those who are reserved and cautious like introverts. This chapter takes some of the information from the previous chapter, delving deeper into the more difficult aspects of social dynamics, including conflict resolution, bullying (physical and relational), and anger management.

Introverts are drained by intense emotional reactions, even their own. Faced with the sensory overload that can come from social interactions, many introverts become overwhelmed. As I've discussed previously, this can lead to increased agitation as the introvert struggles to regain a sense of equilibrium. Add to this scenario the intensity of emotions that often accompany social conflicts and similar situations and introverted children are pushed over the edge, resulting too frequently in behavioral explosions of one form or another. Helping the introvert develop the social skills necessary to navigate difficult social situations, as well as understanding the differences between how introverts react to conflict versus their extroverted counterparts, is key to reducing the chances of explosive behavior.

Introverts are predisposed to seek calm. Rooted in their hard wiring, this need for understanding and peace causes most introverts to pull away from conflict. As their stress levels and the demands for social attention increase, introverts will often withdraw emotionally from social turmoil.

Extroverts, on the other hand, engage. Their natural fight or flight reaction kicks in, pushing them toward an almost aggressive response to stress and conflict. The opposing forces of the need of the extrovert to engage and that of the introvert to withdraw can often result in unbalanced social exchanges that can escalate into explosive pouts. Even when introverts are in conflict with other introverts, the intensity of their emotions can create disharmony that increases both stress and frustration, resulting in negative behavioral exchanges.

How can parents help redirect this behavior and teach introverts the skills needed to better navigate the normal social difficulties that can occur in any relationship? I think it begins with helping introverted children understand the nature of their emotions, recognizing which types of intense emotions impact them and how. Understanding the impact other people's emotions have on your introverts can help them, and you, develop strategies to process that emotion without reacting to it.

Consider this example: An introverted mother of two extroverted girls is continually drained by her job at an up-and-coming technology firm. She comes home, already exhausted, and is confronted by her daughters who are engaged in a heated verbal argument. Unable to process through the intense emotions, the mother yells at both children, adding fuel to the existing fire. Before long the incident has deteriorated into a smaller version of WWIII.

Sound familiar? Most parents I talk to can relate to this in some way. The truth is that most of the drama could have been avoided with a few small interventions: time to regroup prior to the mother coming home, emotional detachment during the argument, and a little time away for everyone.

TIP SHEET 24
Problem Solving 101

❖ Remain calm.

❖ State the problem using "I" statements ("I am feeling . . .").

❖ Allow the other person to state the problem from his perspective.

❖ Stay away from blame and shame.

❖ Brainstorm a solution to the problem.

❖ Decide on the solution and make a plan.

❖ Thank the person for helping to solve the problem.

Once your introverted children understand their emotional hooks, help them practice the stress-busting strategies presented in Chapter 7. Learning to regain a sense of calm is a great way to avoid most conflicts in the first place.

There are times, however, when conflicts occur despite your children's best efforts to avoid them. When this happens, it is important for children to understand how to navigate through the conflict without becoming more drained. Teach them how to listen to others, engage in creative problem-solving techniques, and compromise. These basics of problem solving and conflict management can resolve many of the difficult social situations. The tip sheet on this page reviews the basics of problem solving, skills every introvert needs to learn.

Sometimes sticky situations escalate faster than your introverted child can try to solve the problem. At these times, anger and other negative emotions may spin out of control. It is important for your child to have some strategies to calm himself and diffuse the anger. Teaching your child the strategies listed on page 156, and practicing them frequently, can help your introverted child prevent some of the angry conflicts that can arise between friends.

Empowering your children with specific ways in which to deal with anger, as well as an understanding that intense emotions do happen within social situations, is a great way to help them understand social dynamics more clearly.

TIP SHEET 25

Diffusing Anger

- ❖ Know what triggers your emotions.
- ❖ Take a deep breath and still your thoughts.
- ❖ Count to 10.
- ❖ Walk away.
- ❖ Find a safe person you can always vent to when you are angry.

Anger and aggression often go hand in hand. Anger is the emotion, and aggression is often the action. Aggression is typically defined as a forceful action designed to dominate another. It is one of the most typical components of bullying, one of the hardest social problems facing our schools.

Bullies can be extroverts or introverts. They engage in behavior that is aggressive in nature, designed to overpower a victim, and pervasive. Most bullying is either verbal, like taunting and gossiping both at school and online. Other forms of bullying include relational, when the aggression attacks social connections through ignoring and seclusion, and physical, including property damage and physical aggression. Bullies victimize indiscriminately, meaning anyone is a potential victim. And all of the forms of bullying have the power to inflict significant harm, undermining self-esteem and feelings of safety for the victims.

Teaching your introverted children how to handle a bully can be a challenge. As mentioned previously, most introverts withdraw in the face of aggression and conflict. They have a hard time believing that people can be so unkind. Teaching them that there are people who will not always act fairly or in a kind manner is important, as is teaching specific skills for working with bullies.

Just as important as understanding what a bully is, introverted children need to understand what a bully isn't. Law enforcement typically defines bullying as acts of dominance, in which the perpetrator is trying to exert control over the victim and the victim feels powerless. This is beyond the typical social difficulties kids may experience, beyond taunt-

---

TIP SHEET 26

How to Deal With Bullies

❖ First, clarify what a bully is and is not with your child.

❖ Determine if the school has an anonymous way to report bullying. If it does, allow the child to use that format. If it does not:
   o Determine a "safe" time to talk with the administration of the school.
   o Encourage your child to always report incidents of bullying.

❖ If your child is the victim of bullying, be sure to spend time teaching the child how to work past the negative impact of the bully.

---

ing that can happen on schoolyards across the nation, and beyond a simple conflict between peers. Bullying involves intent, aggression, and dominance.

Take a look at the tip sheet above. Use the strategies to help your child learn what to do when faced with a bully.

It's important that introverted children understand why they need to report acts of bullying. Teach them how and when to intervene. Only in silence does bullying continue. Regaining a sense of safety and empowerment happens when we take action and let go of any shame we are feeling either as victims or witnesses to acts of bullying.

In addition to reporting acts of bullying, it is important for your children to know how to recover. Throughout this book, I have given you tips for teaching introverted children how to deal with stress, improve overall coping strategies, and develop emotional strength and resiliency. These same strategies can help children recover if they are victims to acts of aggression and/or bullying. Remind your children that they can rise above the negative feelings of hurt and shame, that it will get better. You and your children have the ability to regain the feelings of safety that may have been lost. You just need to work together to do it. Learn what it means to bully. Make sure your children don't engage in bullying behavior. Teach them who to talk to if they are bullied or if they witness acts of bullying. By taking action, you and your child can stop the bully's negative impact.

This chapter has been all about difficult social interactions and ways introverted children can smooth out the hard times. Focusing on coping skills, problem solving, and dealing with intense emotions are the best ways you can assist your child in handling the more difficult aspects of relationships.

Class Notes: Teaching Tolerance at School

Bullying and poor social interactions account for a significant amount of the behavioral problems in schools. The PBIS strategies mentioned in other chapters can help bridge the gap with regard to explicitly teaching social skills that both extroverts and introverts need in order to manage their behaviors and interact with peers appropriately.

Another thing teachers can do to create safe classroom environments that promote prosocial behavior is teaching tolerance. This can be done through cultural awareness weeks, "culture walks," and promoting diversity. Increasing awareness of various cultures, as well as breaking down typical stereotypes, helps children increase their tolerance for those who are different in some way. It is important to include learning and socioeconomic diversity, as well as cultural diversity. The tips on page 159 outline ways to teach tolerance in the classroom setting, something critical in today's multicultural world.

Cultural walks, sensitivity training, and diversity awareness work in concert with antibullying programs to promote safer schools for all students. Why not try out some of those strategies in your school?

TIP SHEET 27
Building Tolerance

❖ Start with a safe classroom environment.
❖ Embrace diversity and cultural awareness.
❖ Incorporate sensitivity training and "culture walks" into the curriculum.
❖ Teach prosocial behaviors to students.
❖ Manage stereotypes, including your own.

SOCIAL DILEMMAS Q & A

In addition to social development, many of the parents I work with worry about bullying, conflict resolution, and anger management. The questions that follow focus on some of the difficulties introverted children have when trying to manage their emotions and deal with bullies and other social dilemmas.

My son tends to take a lot from his friends and then will suddenly lash out. As a result, he's often the one getting in trouble even though his behavior is the result of a lot of built-up frustration. How can we as parents help him in these situations?

Introverts typically have a long fuse, internalizing their frustrations rather than dealing with them in the open like most extroverts do. As a result, they often appear to not be bothered by others until they become explosive related to their pent-up frustration. The best way to help introverts regulate their emotional responses with more balance is to help them become more aware of what bothers them, learn how to express their needs to others in socially appropriate ways, and learn how to respond when they are on overload. One way to manage some of this is through the development of an emotional vocabulary, or a way of talking about

---

TIP SHEET 28

Developing an Emotional Vocabulary

- ❖ Work with your child to define his or her emotions in terms of how the behavior looks.
- ❖ Come up with a word to describe each emotion.
- ❖ Define the meaning of the words.
- ❖ Use the word(s) as a cue when the child is unable to discuss emotions.
- ❖ Encourage your child to openly discuss his or her emotions.

---

their emotions. By learning how to talk about emotions, the words to use and when to talk about them, introverted children can begin to learn to express themselves when overloaded. Take a look at the tips on page 160 for quick strategies to teach an emotional vocabulary to children.

Another way to assist introverts in managing their emotions is to teach them to journal or use similar strategies to stay in touch with their emotional selves. Teaching children to regulate their emotions before they reach the point of overload is the best gift you can give your introverts.

What strategies should I be teaching my child to help with his social interactions, especially when there are conflicts?

Most introverted children avoid conflicts like the plague. Unwilling to interrupt others when they are speaking or risk humiliation through confrontation, introverts often wind up saying nothing and internalizing the problems rather than seeking a resolution to the conflict. Fortunately, there is a lot parents can do to assist introverts as they learn how to problem solve social situations.

First, remind your introverted children that conflicts should never be dealt with when everyone is angry. Teach your children to take a break and calm down prior to discussing the problems. Finally, go through the conflict resolution and problem-solving tips throughout the chapter. Use these strategies with your introverted children to teach them how to successfully navigate through difficult social patches.

I really want my introverted daughter to have more friends. Is this wrong?

Similar to concerns in the previous chapter, this question speaks to the overriding concern many parents have with friendship and the number of friends their children have. Being concerned with your daughter's social life is normal. We, as parents, always want our children to develop strong and supportive friendships to help them throughout their lives. However, focusing on the number of friends someone acquires is, in my opinion, a misguided concern, often occurring when extroverted parents have introverted children.

Extroverts typically establish many friendships. Not all of these relationships are deep, but to the extrovert, it works. Introverts don't develop a significant number of friendships. They tend to build one or two friendships at a time, focusing on the depth of the relationship and not the number of friendships.

One style of friendship development is not better than the other. What's important is whether or not the relationships are meeting the needs of the child. The degree to which your child has meaningful relationships from which she can derive support is the appropriate focus for parents.

It seems like some cultures don't view introversion as a bad thing. Is this true?

Yes, many Eastern cultures, especially those in Asia, find the extroversion attributes celebrated in Western culture distasteful. In those cultures, being reserved, quiet, and calm are the attributes held in high regard. This difference in ideals is a reminder that although the attributes of temperament are determined by our hard wiring, whether or not those attributes are held in high regard relates directly to specific cultural definitions.

Bullying is a big deal in schools now. Are introverted students targeted more than extroverted students? Is there something that I can do as a teacher to reduce this?

Most researchers agree that bullying is indiscriminate when it comes to victims. It does not follow ethnic, economic, or cultural patterns.

Anyone can be the victim of bullying. The key to preventing bullying from occurring is focusing on positive behavior interventions and supports and establishing safe environments for children. Be aware of students who do not appear to have friends, students who demonstrate sudden changes in behavior, and students who suddenly avoid other students. These could be indicators of bullying and should be addressed. Additionally, teach children how to report bullying behavior they may witness or experience. Children need to know specifically how to act in light of bullying in order to take action.

In a Nutshell . . .

Big Ideas

❖ Intense emotions present large energy drains for introverts.

❖ Introverts are easily humiliated in many socially intense situations.

❖ Learning conflict management skills and creative problem-solving skills is important for introverts when navigating social difficulties.

❖ Developing an emotional vocabulary, as well as learning the art of journaling, enables introverts to discuss their feelings in some way.

❖ Bullying is a problem for all people. Introverts, in particular, may struggle with knowing how to deal with a bully.

❖ Learning how to set and maintain boundaries is very important for introverts.

❖ Tolerance is the key to creating safe environments for all children, including introverts.

Supplemental Pages

chapter 15

Creativity, Technology, and Building on Strengths

"The day my parents let me get a phone with texting was the day I felt like I could finally connect with others. It is just so much easier to text than it is to call someone on the phone."—Amani, Age 14

I've spent the better part of the book talking about ways that introverts can strengthen their understanding of introversion, develop the positive aspects of their temperament, and minimize the potential drawbacks to introversion. This is the foundation for self-reliance and empowerment.

Developing authentic self-reliance requires a basis of personal understanding and the development of resiliency. Several chapters and strategies gave insight as to how you, as parents, can help foster this in your children. Developing strong self-efficacy, mastering specific social competencies in the areas of social interactions, and learning emotional control all contribute to the development of a healthy sense of self. Additionally, exploring interests that build on the strengths of introversion can foster both self-reliance and self-actualization.

Creativity is a natural area of competency for most introverted people. I am using the broadened sense of creativity in this context, inclusive of more than the arts and artistic endeavors. I am referring to creativity defined as the ability to move past traditional ideas and thoughts and create something new built from the old—innovation.

Creativity can apply to any content or subject area, and really refers to the process by which something new is generated. Author Julia Cameron (1992) referred to the creative process as a natural force, requiring periods of solitude, stillness, and contemplation. Sound like any particular type of temperament we know?

Introverts are particularly well-suited to a creative path. In fact, I would suggest that all introverts require opportunities for creative contemplation in order to stay balanced. This creativity may happen through a school-based activity or through extracurricular involvement. Whatever the case, introverts require time to creatively reflect as much as they require opportunities for solitude in general. The tip sheet on page 167 explores traditional and nontraditional ways to include creativity into the introverted child's life.

Nurturing creativity requires nothing more than an inquisitive mind. Ask your child questions about the world and how things work. Encourage her to push deeper into areas of interest. This will not be hard for the introvert, as it is a natural function of her hardwiring. My daughters and their friends are a great example of this. Raised to embrace their naturally creative minds, they infuse creativity into everything from making up word games on the way to school, to finding creative solutions for juggling homework with extra activities.

In the early chapters, I spoke about the need for structure and routine for the introvert. Although it is true that both foster a sense of safety for the child, they can also stifle creative efforts. Introduce periods of unscheduled time in which children are free to explore and create. This will balance both the need for safety and the freedom and space required for creation.

Speaking of creation and innovation, I have not discussed the impact of technology on introverted children. More than another tool that can

---

TIP SHEET 29
Encouraging Creativity

Introverted children are particularly adept at creative activities in a multitude of domains. Adding opportunities for creative expression throughout the day is a great way to encourage and build on this area of natural strength for the introvert. The list below includes daily activities designed to enhance creativity:

❖ Have your child read something new or unfamiliar, such as a book in a new genre or on an unexplored topic, every day.

❖ Ask the question "what else?" often.

❖ Have your child come up with five new ways to use familiar objects every day.

❖ Play creative word games and puzzles often.

❖ Make a "creation" box filled with any art supplies, paper towel tubes, and other objects. Pull out the box whenever your child needs something to do. The box can provide entertainment beyond the familiar video games and TV shows.

❖ The next time your child wants a new game, have them make one.

❖ Look for ways for your child to be creative every day.

---

enhance creativity and "playtime," our modern world has also provided our introverted population with a type of buffer against the emotional energy that often accompanies large groups of people or the particularly active extrovert.

Technology such as social media and texting have enabled introverted people to connect more than ever. Without the constant energy drain that occurs in face-to-face encounters, these digital versions of connecting enable the introverted child to appear more "extroverted," managing multiple relationships, connecting with greater frequency, and increasing connections in previously unexplored social domains.

Take a moment to consider the digital activities and technology your introvert interacts with on a daily basis. The worksheet on page 169 highlights only a few of the social media sites and types of technology many children use on a regular basis. Use the blank lines on the chart to add those things specific to your children.

Social networking and the use of technology are good things for the most part, enabling introverts to connect in new ways. However, social media does have drawbacks, including being highly addicting. Psychologists are just beginning to study the impact of social networking, but early research suggests that it can be more addicting than alcohol or drug use (Chou, Condron, & Belland, 2005). For introverts in particular, the sudden ability to widely connect on a social level without the face-to-face interaction and energy drain can wind up being overwhelming, as less attention is paid to their need for solitude. To know whether or not social media and technology has become a "problem" for your child, look again at Worksheet 8 (see page 169). Start keeping track of the number of hours your child spends interacting online, as well as the amount of texting and when it is occurring. What do you notice? Is there significantly more time spent in online relationships than with face-to-face interactions? Is technology interfering with daily functioning and sleep? These could be indicators that balance is needed. The tip sheet on page 170 provides some suggestions to help your introverted child, or any child, balance his or her use of technology.

No conversation about technology and the Internet would be complete without some mention of online safety. Teaching your child to be safe online does not mean completely restricting access to technology. As I mentioned previously, there are a significant number of positive benefits to be gained when introverted children have access to and use technology. And, like it or not, we live in a digital age. Children are going to utilize technology and be online. The key is to teach them, and ourselves, about being safe.

Safety in a digital age begins with a little reality check about privacy. The minute anyone puts information online, it is subject to potential theft. Additionally, things you say online cannot be unsaid, even when you delete the words. Teaching children about this reality is vital as they begin to use the Internet more frequently. Become educated about privacy settings on websites. Know your children's passwords. Teach them

WORKSHEET 8
Technology for Introverts

Take a moment to complete the chart, indicating the types of technology your child uses, why he or she uses it, and how frequently it is used.

Type of Technology	Purpose	Amount of Use
Computer		
iPod		
Tablet		
Mobile phone		
E-mail		
Texting		
Social media sites		

TIP SHEET 30
The Tech Trap

❖ Help your child focus on personal relationships as well as social media.
❖ Turn off computers, cell phones, and tablets at night.
❖ "Unplug" the family from the Internet one day a month.
❖ Never text, chat, or e-mail and drive. Make sure your children see a good example in your behavior.

to change them frequently. All of these measures will help keep them safe online.

Privacy isn't the only online concern. Relationships are not the same online as they are face-to-face. People can lie and deceive, portraying themselves as something they are not. As introverts begin to connect online, it is important that they understand this and be cautious. I say this not to dissuade you from allowing, or even encouraging, online communication. I say it merely because it is something to be aware of.

Finally, I would be remiss if I didn't mention texting and driving. Although most parents and kids understand the dangers, the research is clear—teens continue to text or e-mail while driving. So do adults. Make sure you aren't one of them. Teach your children to put the phone away while driving. Practice safe habits as well. It is the only way to prevent texting-related accidents.

Class Notes: Technology, The Great Equalizer

This chapter focused on developing the positive attributes of introversion, building creativity and the use of technology. It seemed fitting that the section on the classroom should also focus on technology. We live in an exciting time in which technology enables our students to engage with curriculum in new and exciting ways. For the introverted learner, technology can be particularly helpful in allowing the introvert a venue in which to develop creativity and build connections, without getting overstimulated through social connection.

Apps for iPads and other tablets, computer programs such as Google Docs and PowerPoint, and video applications have all become more commonplace in the classroom, allowing introverted learners additional tools to enable deep levels of exploration with content as well as meaningful ways to connect to the material and demonstrate mastery.

One of the more creative uses of technology I have seen recently is the use of classroom blogs. Specific sites are used to ensure student safety online while also providing opportunities for students to engage in meaningful conversations and demonstrate learning. For the introvert, the blog and similar forums can give him or her a buffer against the energy transfer that can happen with "in person" social interactions, and yet still allow opportunities for meaningful connections, something introverts thrive on. Blogs and forums also allow for collaborative efforts within the context of individual innovation, another thing that would be of great benefit to the introverted learner.

FOSTERING INDEPENDENCE Q&A

All parents want their children to grow up to be strong, self-reliant adults. Developing independence starts in childhood, happening as the result of a person's experiences over time. The following questions were chosen from several of my parenting workshops and address some of the more common areas of concern that can impact the overall development of independence and self-reliance.

I often don't realize there is an issue with my son until it has built to huge proportions—how do we help him understand and express his feelings better?

Most introverts hold their emotions inside, refusing to discuss things that are troubling them until they become explosive. At this point, it is often too late for parents to intervene. Reread the tips throughout Chapter 5, paying attention to helping your introverted son learn how to recognize and regulate his emotions. Learning to manage himself in this way is vital as he grows and develops. It will help him build his emotional intelligence and enable him to strengthen the positive attributes of introversion, including self-reflection.

What are the best ways to help an introvert realize how amazing he or she is?

Most parents want their children to recognize their inner strengths. This is particularly true with introverted children, as they are frequently hyperfocusing on their mistakes, overthinking every misstep in the hopes of not repeating mistakes. Reinforce strategies for relaxation presented earlier in the book. Teach your introverted children to spend a little time focusing on positive qualities they possess. Help them list out their strengths, if necessary. Provide regular praise on things your children do well. Make sure you also give them the message of unconditional high regard just for being alive. These things will all reinforce positive self-esteem in your introverted child.

My introverted daughter is always comparing herself to her extroverted sister. I am worried that her self-esteem is low. What can I do to help her?

Comparisons among siblings is normal and not necessarily indicative of a problem. I recommend spending individual time with each child, focusing on developing individual relationships as well as the larger family dynamic. In this way, you can help your introverted child see her own unique strengths. Be careful to not add fuel to the sibling rivalry fire by engaging in your own comparisons. This will only cause discord between the children and strain the family unit. Allow each child the space to become authentic and develop unique interests.

I heard that introverts do better with technology-assisted communication (i.e., texting, chatting, IM). Is this true? Why?

The research regarding introversion and technology is only in the very early stages. However, speaking as an adult introvert, I can tell you that texting and chatting has turned me from a recluse into a social butterfly. No, seriously, chatting and texting online has enabled me and my introverted child to connect in ways not previously available, all without the typical energy drain that accompanies social interactions in person. This allows me to connect more frequently and for longer periods of time. As I work with more and more introverted individuals, this pattern seems to be true for them as well. The only drawback? I still need periods of solitude in order to renew. Without the constant energy drain from face-to-face interactions, I am more likely to overextend myself and crash. Balance is the key, one many introverts struggle with when it comes to social media usage.

My son is very creative. He is also an introvert. He often refuses to share his art with anyone, saying that it isn't "good enough." How can help him develop his art and gain confidence enough to share it with others?

Ah yes, the familiar perfectionism trap. This is a common problem for many creative individuals, particularly creative introverts who engage in excessive thinking and contemplation about their artwork. Toning down the inner critic begins with an understanding of how the creative process works, followed by the teaching of strategies to help your son overcome his perfectionism. Don't focus too much on the sharing of his art. Switch the focus, instead, to embracing his inner artist, developing his skills, and taming the inner critic. These strategies can help your son develop his talent. The rest will come as his confidence grows.

As a teacher, I really want to foster independence for my students. Is there a way I should do this with introverted children?

The good thing about introverted learners is that they are very independent. That said, there are a few things you can do strengthen their autonomy. Start with a safe and predictable classroom. Then, allow some freedom with regard to the depth of study of some topics. Introverts thrive when they are allowed to study high-interest content at a deeper level. Build creativity into your curriculum and encourage technology usage. All of these things will foster independence and creative thinking as your introverted students interact more fully with the curriculum.

In a Nutshell . . .

Big Ideas

* Being authentic is challenging for all children.
* Resiliency and understanding are the cornerstones to personal fulfillment.
* Technology provides introverts with increased opportunities to be social.
* Technology has some risks for the introvert, including lack of balance between the social needs and energy drain.
* Parents and educators play a role in helping children embrace their inner selves.
* Creative venues are good outlets for introverts as they discover their own voice.

Supplemental Pages

* Tip Sheet 29: Encouraging Creativity—page 167
* Worksheet 8: Technology for Introverts—page 169
* Tip Sheet 30: The Tech Trap—page 170

chapter 16

In Their Own Words
Moving From Shame to Empowerment

I've had the joy of working with many children over my years in education and during my training workshops. Sometimes I am afforded the luxury of being able to work with children over the course of a few years.

About 6 years ago, I met a young girl who struggled greatly in school, resulting in many emotional outbursts and a reluctance to attend. I was able to work with her intermittently over 2 years. We worked on understanding temperament and building resiliency. By the end of the second year, the girl attended school regularly without the emotional outbursts.

I changed job roles at that time and did not see the girl again until I ran into her at one of my focus groups. She and I had an opportunity to catch up on her life. The story below is her story of accepting her introversion and seeing the strength in her temperament. Her name has been changed, as well as the specific details of her story. But the theme of accepting one's introversion remains intact.

School was a scary place for me when I was younger. We moved to a new town and I started a new school in fourth grade. Although I was excited to start school, I was very afraid. The class smelled like mildew and the bell that indicated the start of class was loud, as were the announcements that also interrupted the morning schedule. The school seemed to be stuffed with too many students, and I felt crowded in class and at recess.

Every day I went to school, feeling more and more anxious. I cried whenever the teacher called on me, struggled when the routine changed, and failed to make any meaningful friendships. I still loved to learn, but as the days moved on, even the academic part of school was no longer something I was looking forward to.

Things were just as hard at home. I hated spending time with my mom. She always asked me about school. I never knew what to say, so I said nothing. But she wasn't satisfied with that. So she'd ask again and again, until finally I'd just yell an answer to her.

After several months, I started to see a counselor at the school. We did some questionnaires together to start. She asked a lot of questions about how I felt when there was too much noise or when the other students spoke loudly. She also asked about what I liked to do at home when I was alone and what kinds of things made me feel relaxed.

After all of the questions, the counselor told me that I was probably an introvert. She explained that as an introvert, I was overwhelmed by things like strong scents or loud sounds. She also said that my anxieties and apprehension were likely related to the introversion, as it seemed like I was overwhelmed.

Over the next several months, we tried different strategies to help me. I started getting more sleep. I learned to ask for "alone" time and started bringing a book to school to help me anytime I just needed to "escape" for a little while. My counselor worked with my teacher to allow me to go to the library at lunch, giving me a quiet place to decompress. She also worked with my parents and explained to them that I needed time right when I came home to relax—time without questions or pressures.

One of the things that helped the most was learning to take a "mini-vacation," as my counselor called it. She taught me how to visualize myself in the mountains (my favorite place) whenever I felt like I needed to disappear for a little while. And she taught me how to explain to others what it meant to be introverted.

It took several months before I stopped feeling overwhelmed. But once I started learning these techniques, things got better.

It has been 4 years since I worked with that counselor. I am in high school now. I no longer have emotional meltdowns at school, nor do I struggle with my need for solitude. I've come to find out that a lot of others need downtime, too. It isn't something to be ashamed of and it doesn't mean there is anything wrong with me.

I've also learned that there are a lot of good things about being an introvert. I can concentrate a lot longer than most of my friends. I don't rush my artwork, nor do I need to constantly be around other people in order to feel "whole"—something that some of my more extroverted friends struggle with. I have leadership qualities and feel things very deeply.

Most of all, I am no different than everyone else. I want friends who understand me. I have dreams of going to college and finding a successful career. Yes, there are many things that still make me uncomfortable: talking to strangers, for example, or the first day of school. But I know that my extroverted friends struggle with things too.

In the end, I have a lot more in common with my friends than I have differences. Temperament is just one of the few differences. It is neither good nor bad. I am neither proud nor ashamed of being an introvert. It is just one aspect of who I am and how I interact with the world.

In this story, one teen shared her experiences with being an introvert. She learned how to avoid becoming overwhelmed and how to recognize her strengths. She also learned what temperament means for her.

Everyone's experience with temperament is unique in some way. What's important is that we help our children embrace their own unique way of interacting with the world, enhancing the positive attributes of temperament and working around those attributes that can become obstacles. It's my hope that the strategies presented throughout the book have helped in some way as you work with your introverted children.

Looking to
the Future

We've covered the major domains of life for your children—home, school, and friends—and examined the potential pitfalls that can happen with introverts. Throughout the chapters, there have been charts, worksheets, and tip sheets to help provide practical advice and strategies to enhance the lives of your children.

I hope you have found the information helpful as you work with your introverted child. Maybe you have learned some things about yourself as well. As you look now to the future and the impact introversion has across the lifespan, take a moment to reflect on your new opinions about introversion overall, and compare them to the feelings you had when you started the book. Take a couple of minutes to answer the questionnaire on page 180 and think about what you will take with you as you continue to influence and support your children.

QUESTIONNAIRE 6

Ideas About Introverts, Revisited

1. After reading the book, I now define an extroverted person as . . . (*complete the sentence*).

2. After reading the book, I now define an introverted person as . . . (*complete the sentence*).

3. I understand how temperament factors into my household now.
   ❑ *True*　　　　❑ *False*

4. My introverted child's best strengths are . . . (*complete the sentence*).

5. My child's biggest obstacles are . . . (*complete the sentence*).

6. I am most worried about my introverted child in the area of . . . (*complete the sentence*).

Once you are finished, take a moment to reflect on your answers and consider the following questions: Has this book helped clarify your understanding of your child? Do you feel like you can help your child with the issues that may arise? Are there remaining things you worry about? Take a moment to write down your thoughts regarding temperament and your goals for this book.

Final Thoughts

Raising children is challenging. Most of the time, we feel over-whelmed with the task—both related to our temperament and related to how our child's temperament interacts with our own. We worry about the difficulties our introverted child may face in a world that heralds extroversion as the ideal. We wonder if we have done all that we can to help our child recognize his or her own gifts as an introvert.

Yes, parenting is a difficult job.

It's my hope that the strategies I've provided will give you some respite, some understanding of the introverted children in your life. And maybe some insight into you or your spouse.

The strategies presented probably sound easy to accomplish. The tip sheets may seem like things you have heard a hundred times before. I caution you not to assume that "easy sounding" is easy to master. Within the simple wording of the strategy is a technique that often takes time to learn to execute well. Even with perfect execution, they may not always work. There will be times when the introversion, yours or your child's, gets the better of you. Things will go wrong. They just will.

I say this not to discount you or the book, but to assure you that when things go wrong, when life's curveballs get to be too much and nothing seems to help, it is my hope that the things you've picked up in the book will help you remember that life is about these teachable moments. It is about the times when you get to start over, try again, and keep working.

Should you reach a time when you feel like you've failed at parent-ing, a time when you are convinced that you've somehow "hurt" your child by not being effective in your parenting, I want you to remember something—you will not fail so long as you continue to try. Help your children understand what it means to be introverted. Help him or her develop strategies to build on the positive aspects of introversion and negate the more negative ones. Teach him or her how to find balance when things get overwhelming. Do this, and you will never fail.

You will eventually have more successes on this journey than perceived failures. You will see your child embrace his or her introversion and develop his or her own ways of coping, ways that enhance his or her strengths. When you see these moments, take some time to celebrate. You both deserve it.

And then, send me an e-mail. I would love to hear from you about your journey. Contact me with your own stories and suggestions. I can be reached via e-mail at Christine@christinefonseca.com or on my many social networking sites. Together we can help our children embrace the truth of who they are and build on their attributes.

Recommended Resources

Information related to temperament has grown over the past decade, but good resources can still be hard to find. Below is a list of my favorite reads dealing with temperament, introversion, parenting, education, and some of the difficulties parents face

General Information on Temperament and Introversion

Here are a few of my favorite titles related to temperament. Each one brings its own unique spin on the topic:

1. *Quiet: The Power of Introverts in a World That Can't Stop Talking* by Susan Cain (Crown, 2012)—A thoughtful and comprehensive analysis of the biological and cultural background of introversion and what can be done to help introverts find their voice.

2. *The Introvert Advantage: How To Thrive in an Extrovert World* by Marti Olsen Laney (Publishing, 2002)—A good overview of the neuroscience behind temperament, as well as specific guidance for thriving as an introvert in today's society.

3. *The Introvert's Way: Living a Quiet Life in a Noisy World* by Sophia Dembling (Perigee, 2012)—A good look at introversion in a positive light, filled with strategies to enhance the power that comes with introversion.

General Parenting

There are very few parenting books related to temperament and introversion. Here are a few I have found helpful over the years. I have also included some related to giftedness, as gifted children often possess traits similar to introversion.

1. *The Hidden Gifts of the Introverted Child: Helping Your Child Thrive in an Extroverted World* by Marti Olsen Laney (Workman, 2005)—Using the concepts in her book, *The Introvert Advantage*, Laney tailors the conversation for parents.

2. *A Parent's Guide to Gifted Children* by James T. Webb, Janet L. Gore, Edward R. Amend, and Arlene R. DeVries (Great Potential Press, 2007)—A comprehensive parenting book that covers the characteristics of giftedness, emotional intensity, and good parenting techniques.

3. *Parenting from the Inside Out: How a Deeper Self-Understanding Can Help You Raise Children Who Thrive* by Daniel Siegel and Mary Hartzell (Putnam, 2003)—A great resource for understanding the connection between self-awareness, self-actualization, and parenting.

4. *Nurture by Nature: Understand Your Child's Personality Type—and Become a Better Parent* by Paul D. Tieger and Barbara Barron-Tieger (Little, Brown, 1997)—A look at the need to understand the psychological aspects of temperament as a foundation for effective parenting.

Working With Intense Behaviors

In the early days of identifying introversion, much emphasis was placed on the emotional intensity and high reactivity that can accompany introverted children. I've included a few titles relating to emotional intensity to help when dealing with particularly intense behaviors.

1. *Emotional Intensity in Gifted Students: Helping Kids Cope With Explosive Feelings* by Christine Fonseca (Prufrock Press, 2010)—I wrote this book to address the nature of emotional intensity and giftedness. The book is filled with practical strategies to assist parents and educators.

2. *101 Success Secrets for Gifted Kids* by Christine Fonseca (Prufrock Press, 2011)—I wrote this book specifically for gifted children ages 8–12 to give them the tools needed to learn to manage the intensity of their emotions related to their giftedness.

3. *Living With Intensity* edited by Susan Daniels and Michael M. Piechowski (Great Potential Press, 2009)—This book provides an excellent basis in Dabrowski's theories for those wishing for more information in this area.

4. *Smart Teens' Guide to Living With Intensity: How to Get More Out of Life and Learning* by Lisa Rivero (Great Potential Press, 2010)—This is a nice book for teens with additional strategies for living an intense life.

Anxiety/Depression

As mentioned in the book, when introversion is unbalanced, it can result in problems with depression and anxiety. Many of the techniques I've presented to help introverted children thrive involve the management of anxiety responses. Some additional resources when dealing with these types of difficulties include the following:

1. *Anxiety-Free Kids: An Interactive Guide for Parents and Children* by Bonnie Zucker (Prufrock Press, 2008)—This is a terrific guide for children and parents dealing with anxiety.

2. *The Anxiety Cure for Kids: A Guide for Parents* by Elizabeth DuPont Spencer, Robert L. DuPont, and Carolyn M. DuPont

(Wiley, 2003)—A great resource for parents dealing with significantly anxious children. Although the book is geared toward those children diagnosed with anxiety disorders, the strategies will work with less severe cases, or cases involving gifted children as opposed to children diagnosed with an anxiety disorder.

3. *What To Do When Good Isn't Good Enough: The Real Deal on Perfectionism: A Guide for Kids* by Thomas S. Greenspon (Free Spirit, 2007)—A good resource for younger children, providing lots of practical strategies.

Bullying

Bullying is difficult enough for any child to live with. But when the child in question is introverted, dealing with a bully can be particularly problematic. Here is a list of books related to bullying that I have found particularly helpful:

1. *The Bully, The Bullied, and The Bystander: From Preschool to High School—How Parents and Teachers Can Help Break the Cycle of Violence* by Barbara Coloroso (Harper, 2009)—An outstanding explanation of the bullying triangle, with practical strategies to end the cycle of violence.

2. *Girl Wars: 12 Strategies That Will End Female Bullying* by Cheryl Dellasega and Charisse Nixon (Fireside, 2003)—An excellent resource for relational aggression and other forms of female bullying.

Education

As discussed throughout the book, introverts learn differently from extroverts. They require different types of structures and approaches.

Below is a list of resources that address meeting the unique needs of diverse classrooms, including those with a variety of temperaments.

1. "Introversion: A Misunderstood 'Individual Difference' Among Students" by Arnold Henjum (*Education*, 1982, Vol. 103)

2. "How Introverts Versus Extroverts Approach Small-Group Argumentative Discussions" by Michael Nussbaum (*The Elementary School Journal*, 2002, Vol. 102)

3. *Handbook of Positive Behavior Support* edited by Wayne Sailor, Glen Dunlap, George Sugai, & Rob Horner (Springer, 2010)—An excellent reference book for all aspects of developing Schoolwide Positive Behavior Supports.

4. *Responding to Problem Behaviors in Schools: The Behavior Education Program* (2nd ed.) by Deanne A. Crone, Leanne S. Hawken, & Robert H. Horner (Guilford Press, 2010)—Another outside resource for educators looking to build strong positive supports to problem behaviors in schools.

Miscellaneous Resources

Here are some final resources to cover a variety of topics that may arise in a child's life:

1. *Calming the Family Storm: Anger Management for Moms, Dads, and All The Kids* by Gary D. McKay and Steven A. Maybell (Impact Publishers, 2004)—An excellent book full of practical strategies for anger management for all members of the household.

2. *Staying Connected to Your Teenager: How to Keep Them Talking to You and How to Hear What They're Really Saying* by Michael Riera (Da Capo Press, 2003)—A great book to help parents stay connected to the ever-changing world of their teens.

Particularly good when your child is reluctant to talk related to her introversion.

3. *7 Things Your Teenager Won't Tell You: And How To Talk About Them Anyway* by Jennifer Marshall Lippincott and Robin M. Deutsch (Ballantine, 2005)—A book full of the "hard things" and how to talk to your kids about them.

References

Cameron, J. (1992). *The artist's way.* New York, NY: Putnam.

Cattell, R. B., Eber, H. W., & Tatsuoka, M. (1980). *Handbook for the Sixteen Personality Facor Questionnaire.* Champaign, IL: Institute for Personality and Ability.

Chou, C., Condron, L., & Belland, J. C. (2005). A review of the research on internet addiction. *Educational Psychology Review, 17,* 363–388.

Eysenck, H. (1967). *The biological basis of personality.* Springfield, IL: Thomas Publishing.

Fonseca, C. (2010). *Emotional intensity in gifted students: Helping kids cope with explosive feelings.* Waco, TX: Prufrock Press.

Goleman, D. (1998). *Working with emotional intelligence.* New York, NY: Bantum.

Henjum, A. (1982). Introversion: A misunderstood "individual difference" among students. *Education, 103,* 39–43.

Jung, C. G. (1971). *Psychological types: The collected works of C. G. Jung, Vol. 6.* (R. F. Hull, Ed., & H. G. Baynes, Trans.) Princeton, NY: Princeton University Press.

Kagan, J., & Snidman, N. (2004). *The long shadow of temperament.* Cambridge, MA: Harvard University Press.

Laney, M. O. (2002). *The introvert advantage: How to thrive in an extrovert world.* New York, NY: Workman Publishing.

Laney, M. O. (2005). *The hidden gifts of the introverted child: Helping your child thrive in an extroverted world.* New York, NY: Workman Publishing.

Nussbaum, E. M. (2002). How introverts versus extroverts approach small-group argumentative discussions. *The Elementary School Journal, 102,* 183–197.

Prince-Embury, S. (2005). *Resiliency Scale for Adolescence: A profile of personal strengths.* San Antonio, TX: Pearson Education.

Segal, N. L. (1999). *Entwined lives: Twins and what they tell us about human behavior.* New York, NY: Dutton.

Sword, L. (2000). *The gifted introvert.* Retrieved from http://www.starjump.com.au/media/Papers%20%20Articles/The%20Gifted%20Introvert%20by%20Lesley%20Sword_.pdf

Thompson, E. (2008). Development and validation of an international English big five mini markers. *Personality and Individual Differences, 45,* 542–548.

About the Author

Critically acclaimed nonfiction and YA author Christine Fonseca believes that writing is a great way to explore humanity. Using her training and expertise as an educational psychologist, Ms. Fonseca is dedicated to helping children of all ages find their voice in the world. Her titles include *Emotional Intensity in Gifted Students, 101 Success Secrets for Gifted Kids,* and the recently released *The Girl Guide.*

In addition to her nonfiction titles, Ms. Fonseca is the author of several young adult novels including the psychological thriller, *Transcend,* and the Gothic romance, the Requiem series, featuring *Lacrimosa, Libera Me,* and *Dominus.* She has also penned several short stories including "Dies Irae" and "Enigma."

When she's not writing or spending time with her family, she can be found sipping too many skinny vanilla lattes at her favorite coffee house or playing around on Facebook and Twitter. For more information about Christine Fonseca or her books, visit her website: http://christinefonseca. com.